I0711794

THE HEALING VORTEX WITHIN

FORTY-FOUR PORTALS TO AWAKEN YOUR SELF-HEALING SUPERPOWERS

HEATHER L. HOBSON, PSYD

BALBOA.PRESS

A DIVISION OF HAY HOUSE

Copyright © 2022 Heather L. Hobson.

All rights reserved. No part of this book may be used or reproduced by any means, graphic, electronic, or mechanical, including photocopying, recording, taping or by any information storage retrieval system without the written permission of the author except in the case of brief quotations embodied in critical articles and reviews.

Balboa Press books may be ordered through booksellers or by contacting:

Balboa Press
A Division of Hay House
1663 Liberty Drive
Bloomington, IN 47403
www.balboapress.com
844-682-1282

Because of the dynamic nature of the Internet, any web addresses or links contained in this book may have changed since publication and may no longer be valid. The views expressed in this work are solely those of the author and do not necessarily reflect the views of the publisher, and the publisher hereby disclaims any responsibility for them.

The author of this book does not dispense medical advice or prescribe the use of any technique as a form of treatment for physical, emotional, or medical problems without the advice of a physician, either directly or indirectly. The intent of the author is only to offer information of a general nature to help you in your quest for emotional and spiritual well-being. In the event you use any of the information in this book for yourself, which is your constitutional right, the author and the publisher assume no responsibility for your actions.

Any people depicted in stock imagery provided by Getty Images are models, and such images are being used for illustrative purposes only.
Certain stock imagery © Getty Images.

Print information available on the last page.

ISBN: 979-8-7652-2593-6 (sc)
ISBN: 979-8-7652-2595-0 (hc)
ISBN: 979-8-7652-2594-3 (e)

Library of Congress Control Number: 2022905727

Balboa Press rev. date: 03/29/2022

CONTENTS

This book is dedicated to everyone who has ever had a bad experience with traditional therapy or accessing mental health services of any kind. The innate healer within you has been waiting to reconnect to your dormant inner wisdom.

This book is dedicated to those seeking a little something different on the journey of life, healing, and inner work. This book is dedicated to anyone who desires to connect more fully with their soul and the cosmic consciousness of all things.

This book is dedicated to everyone who desperately needs a shift, a new perspective, and tools to begin and maintain the healing and awakening journey. This book is dedicated to my amazing soul sisters and brothers, fellow empaths, rainbow warriors, starseeds, light workers, healers, mystics, poets, cosmic beatniks, wordsmiths, alchemists, artists, and all of you who are coming to realize you too are one of us.

PREFACE

You didn't choose this book. This book chose you.

Welcome to *The Healing Vortex Within: Forty-Four Portals to Awaken Your Self-Healing Superpowers*. If you are reading this book right now, it's because something in your conscious, subconscious, or unconscious energy field pulled you toward it—the inner-healing and awakening vortex of your soul perhaps. That is truly how everything works on this plane of existence; the exact right people, places, and things find us at the exact right time in the exact right way. I believe this now more than ever. Whether you are aware of it or not, your soul's energy is always guiding you, even when it doesn't feel that way.

I share these powerful portals with you, not to get you to think like me or completely subscribe to all these ideas but rather to think for yourself about what portals you want to travel along to find your healing vortex within and to connect more fully to your soul. I also share these personal portals and sacred vortex energies with you to remind you that you're not alone on this healing journey of life. I encourage you to keep an open mind and heart and a willingness to learn with me as we begin this adventure together.

I want to thank you for embarking on this journey of self-discovery, personal growth, deep healing, and the awakening of your inner powers. Most importantly, I want you to thank *yourself.* There is no greater gift you can give yourself than the gift of self-healing and self-awakening. It is no secret that personal growth work is challenging. It can unearth pain that has been long buried within, but it can also reveal buried treasures that make life worth living. After collectively surviving the year 2020 (and 2021), we have witnessed the world united in outrage against global systemic oppression and crimes against humanity.

The year 2020 gave many of us the gift of perfect sight, and the veil has shattered all previous illusions. We have never in history witnessed such a mass collective awakening, collective core healing, and souls ignited with a desire for much better for ourselves and the future of planet Earth. It is no longer simply enough to merely live or exist. While humanity has been suffering from collective amnesia for thousands of years, we are remembering and reactivating our souls' gifts and superpowers. We are remembering why we came here and that we have much bigger soul missions to fulfill. Living a life unhealed is like living each day dead inside. As we heal, we awaken. And as we awaken, we activate more and more powerful energies within ourselves and this planet. The ripple effect of personal inner work is tremendous as you will see along your journey.

I invoke this sacred protection mantra to ensure the highest good for all who experience this book: "In full alignment with the one true God/Source, star families, and my higher self, I infuse this book and all who encounter it with the highest vibrational frequencies of deep healing, awakening, and powerful protection. As these souls travel the portals in this book, please ensure they rediscover their sacred souls' vortex within and activate their self-healing superpowers fully. Thank you for empowering all who read and encounter this book to discover their own unique truth, their own mental, emotional, physical, spiritual, and energetic sovereignty. Thank you for allowing me to bring this book forth from my soul to theirs in service of love and truth. I express my deepest gratitude and love for all souls on earth and beyond through all galaxies, all dimensions, throughout all space and time as a cosmic emissary of love and ascension ambassador. Thank you, thank you, thank you. And so it is done."

Allow me to properly introduce myself. My name is Heather, and I've written this book from my soul for your soul. It has been a labor of love and service. It has also taken me on a wild ride through my inner healing and awakening portals to tap into my unique vortex of self-healing superpowers. This book is a road map of how I did it to help guide you on your unique journey. It has been a healing and awakening process for me as I hope it is for you too to boldly travel through the forty-four portals in this book. Time and time again, I come back to these portals to travel back to myself, back to my soul, and I discover something new every time.

Despite what I might look like on paper, letters behind my name, and such, I am just like you. I love and feel deeply. I seek knowledge, truth, and wisdom. I am learning, growing, and evolving every day. I want to see the world be a better place for everyone. I am not a guru. I am not a master. I am far too honest and humble to ever call myself an expert on anything. A wise person knows you can never truly know everything. By acknowledging how little we know, we are more able to continuously learn and expand to higher dimensions. I am not enlightened, and I still have healing and awakening work to do—which is my life's work—and I look forward to doing it much more now after knowing which portals will take me to my inner superpower vortices. I have been to the depths of hell and back several times. At least now I know my demons' names and how to escape my inner matrix as I fulfill my soul's mission on Earth and dance playfully between fate and free will.

This book is about healing, but more importantly, it is about awakening. This book is about deeply awakening your intuitive voice and the ancient wisdom that resides within your soul. Many of us have been wanting clarity, purpose, and freedom from the shackles of a third-dimensional reality that has created too much pain and suffering for far too long. As we move into a new era, a new decade, a new golden age, as many have said, we know we are capable of so much more than we have been conditioned to believe.

We are beings of light, and we can uplift one another and reclaim our inner capacity to heal and awaken ourselves and the world. This book will open doors and activate portals for you, forty-four to be exact. As you walk through each of these cosmic gateways, please know I walk with you. I have walked, skipped, hopped, and leaped through them all time and time again. I am there cheering you on, empowering you to boldly move through the darkness and reconnect to your soul. I am holding a safe space in the ether for you always.

The forty-four portals in this book are my forty-four favorite doorways into the core self, where all healing and mental health "MacGyvering" of the mind, body, and soul happen. I have an often-radical, weird, eccentric, and innovative way of looking at the world some people are simply not ready to hear. I'm an outsider, and we often need an outside perspective on things to make the radical changes to truly awaken and heal.

Some of you will undoubtedly experience resistance to walking through certain portals; this is to be expected with trying new things or doing the things we know we need to do that are hard or scary. There is no courage without fear. I've been scared and resistant too at times. I get it. *Walk through the portals anyway.* Jump, dance, or meander through them if you like. Dip your toe in, at least, despite how silly or scary it might seem. Take what resonates with you and leave what doesn't as you move through each portal. You are the expert on you. Trust yourself but also challenge yourself. True personal growth happens *outside* the comfort zone. Keep that in mind, and the rest of this book will make more sense and be of optimal use.

In so many ways, we forget that we are all mirrors for one another in this human form, shooting back the exact energy we put out in the world. The forty-four portals in this book are possibly portals you have already heard of or crossed through. You are being called to visit these portals within yet again. Even if you have never done any type of self-healing or inner work, this guide will help show you the way.

It is my greatest hope that by my sharing my personal and professional experiences that many others can unlock the codes to their greatest self-healing superpowers as well. In working through the forty-four portals myself, I have learned more about myself in the past few years than ever before. I have discovered that I am a self-healing superpower galactic priestess sent here to guide you back to your soul. That is my soul's mission, and it truly does light me up to help my clients and readers harness their inner healers, to activate the sacred vortices within their souls, and to awaken their passion for life again. To truly heal and awaken is a profound gift I am grateful to share with you.

I must also mention as sort of a disclaimer that this book isn't a substitute for medical, mental health, or spiritual care. What this book intends to do is to teach you how to see what is beneath whatever you may believe is "wrong" with you. This book intends to give you the tools you need to truly be *you*. This book is a valuable companion tool along your healing and awakening journey and can be used repeatedly throughout your life. You will find that after working through the book once, there might be tune-ups needed from time to time. You might feel called to review certain chapters until something clicks or if you continue to experience challenges in your external or internal worlds. You can even pick one number a day from one to forty-four and use that chapter and the exercises or affirmations as a grounding tool to guide you back to your higher self. You can do this time and time again since we are always learning and evolving, always discovering deeper layers and wisdom within our souls.

Additionally, I feel it's important to emphasize that I'm writing this book from my soul for your soul. My soul doesn't speak the same language as most psychologists, academic writers, or perfectly articulate speakers. My soul does speak the language of deep wisdom and divinely authentic "trillness" (real recognize real). I'm more than qualified in the field of healing arts and in the use of proper grammar, spelling, and psychological jargon, but my soul just wants to keep it *real* with my readers. Cool?

I have a lovely editor and publishing team who have edited this book for errors; however, I have instructed them to leave most of my lingo, slang words, profanity, and other elements that would be considered incorrect by many literary standards. So if you see certain weird, wacky things jump off the page at you, I hope you will smile and be like, "Yep, that sounds just like Dr. Heather." If you know me personally or professionally or have seen any of my work, I probably have said many of these things to you at some point. If you aren't familiar with me, welcome to my magically, weird world of healing and awakening.

ACKNOWLEDGMENTS

First and foremost, I would like to thank the most-high God Source/Prime Creator and the multiverses in which I travel for bringing me the most profound experiences in the last seven years that have brought forth these forty-four portals. The divine has always given me exactly what I needed at exactly the right time, and I am eternally grateful every day to be alive.

I am also infinitely grateful to my family for their love and encouragement and for believing in me when I didn't believe in myself. I would like to send special thanks to my mom, Janet and my sister, Annette; you are my earth angels and biggest supporters and I am eternally grateful to you both. Thank you to my father, Bill, for reminding me to always question authority and to remember that my knowledge is the one thing that can never be taken away from me.

I also extend many thanks to everyone at Balboa Press for their support in getting this book to print and for all the wonderful work they do to support bourgeoning authors. And finally, I want to thank my star brother, Paul the Venetian, of Mount Shasta Spiritual Tours, and fellow ascension ambassador, for his guidance to the ancient portals and vortices of Mount Shasta, Lemuria, and Telos. I am forever grateful for you and your sacred activations that helped me finish this book—and for the wonderful photos you captured for the book cover. Connecting to our ancient past with fellow starseeds is my favorite experience, and I cherish the time I get to spend with you at these sacred sites.

INTRODUCTION

When you work on your personal or collective healing goals, always know the universe is aware of your intentions. Tapping into this universal energy, the energy of the cosmos, will allow you to tap into your own unique inner cosmos and the healing vortex within your soul. Now, at this point, some of you may be saying, "What is this crazy lady really talking about?" Regardless of whatever spiritual or religious beliefs you may or may not have, *this book is for everyone.*

In each chapter of this book, I will walk you through a short and easy-to-apply healing exercise. You can continue to use these healing tools on your own or adapt them to fit your personal growth or spiritual rituals. The book was designed to be used in many ways. You can use the book in a linear fashion, from start to finish, or use it more as an oracle healing guide by choosing a number one through forty-four and opening to that page to see what guidance is in store for you. As we know, healing and awakening aren't linear endeavors. Progress also isn't linear. So give yourself permission to use the book in whatever way feels right to you.

The tools suggested in this book are based on my personal and professional experience with healing and awakening and the field of healing arts. I believe each portal holds a powerful light code for gaining insight, learning, and deep, cellular healing. The whole of the parts is greater than the sum. The forty-four portals combined elevate the potential of healing and awakening. The more consistently you use all the tools in your daily life and routines and self-care rituals, the more benefit you will have. Some of the tools involve self-introspection, thought-provoking questions, journal prompts, and/or healing vortex mantras (in other words, affirmations to reset your brain and create a new powerfully positive parallel reality). Give yourself as much time as you need, especially initially, to look inward, develop awareness within, and work with each portal chapter in whatever way feels useful. There is no timeline; there is no rush.

The more mental, emotional, physical, and spiritual space you give yourself to use the tools, the more empowered you will be.

Why use affirmations or mantras? People use affirmations and mantras for a wide variety of purposes. Affirmations and mantras are synonymous, and for this book, I will solely refer to them as "mantras" moving forward to keep it simple. Mantras are used to reprogram the subconscious mind, which drives 90 percent of everything we say and do (that subconscious mind can be a sneaky saboteur if we don't reprogram it). Using mantras is one of the easiest ways to reprogram our subconscious and conscious minds to be less self-critical and more self-aware. They are positive statements you say aloud and can even chant aloud to further amplify the power of these words. Words are powerful spells that can banish mind control, negative beliefs, unhelpful thoughts, and past trauma conditioning; that is why it is called "spelling."

Words carry immense energy and specific frequencies that can lift us or take us into a deep, dark, dismal abyss depending on what we choose to say or think and the energy behind those words. What we believe about ourselves at a subconscious level has a significant impact on the outcome of events. Beliefs are simply thoughts or mantras we have thought, heard, or told ourselves many times. You can change a thought, you can change a belief, and working with mantras is an easy and effective way to heal and awaken daily. Even more importantly, with every word, statement, or mantra you choose to say, you literally create a new reality or alternate universe for yourself. Would you rather create the reality that you are "broken and life sucks, so why bother?" or the expansive universe that you are "learning and evolving, so maybe this mantra thing is worth a try"? That is the power of your choices, your decisions, even your decision to be reading this book right now.

Quantum physicists, cosmologists, and multiverse mavens like me will tell you that every decision you make creates a parallel reality. And there are other simultaneous realities where you also exist doing the things you didn't choose. This is one of the most intriguing concepts and one of the most mind-bending ones, but for now, all you need to remember is that it is your choice to actively work with the mantras in this book, and it is your choice to decide how and when to use them. I like to use mantras all day, *every* day. I like to say them aloud in funny voices or accents, move around while I say them, or write them down; and I also love to make up my own. I encourage you to find your own unique rhythm with this mantra magic.

Some individuals think mantras are religious and feel hesitant to practice them. They are spiritual, not religious. Every single person has a divine right to create their own spiritual sovereignty, meaning we each have our own unique truth. For some people, their spiritual practices involve working with sound frequencies or playing or listening to music. Does music have a religion? Well, maybe gospel music does (he-he). Music in general is beyond religion, and so are mantras. Nature and the soothing rustling of the redwood trees in the mist are beyond religion as well and deeply spiritual just like mantras. Mantras are cosmic sounds in a zip file. When the right chord is tapped into while playing an instrument, a peaking happens. This is something you will understand as you explore these specific tools.

The formula for the most effective mantras is the following:

1. Mantras begin with "I" or "I am" or "I choose." These prefixes turn mantras into statements of identity. Identity statements are powerful motivators for self-change, and anything you say after "I am," you become.
2. Mantras are positive statements; we want to focus on what we want rather than what we don't want.
3. Mantras must have an emotional charge to optimally work. Infuse the mantras you use with feeling; say them loudly or with a smile on your face, even if that's hard to do. It works if you work it, baby.
4. Mantras are written in the present state as if they are already happening. This is the step people get all bent out of shape about because they feel ridiculous saying something they don't believe is true—*yet*—at least at the conscious level. Most of the negative, automatic thoughts we think aren't true. Thoughts aren't facts, but they do elicit powerful emotional responses and behaviors. Remember: you are reprogramming your mind, body, and spirit; and this process can take time. Be patient.

You are using these healing mantras to rewrite your subconscious mind, to create new neural pathways that support the full activation of your inner badass. It's okay if it feels weird or silly or like it's not working. That is your ego and fear of change talking. But when you repeat mantras as a regular practice, a prime point of presence and power in you is activated, energy is shifted, and you are actively healing and awakening yourself.

For you overachievers or those wanting even more depth to mantra work, you can say them in front of a mirror while looking into your eyes. This practice can be very uncomfortable at first, speaking from personal experience. I hated mirror work initially, but then I realized it was because I had been neglecting the relationship with myself *big-time*, and I noticed I was holding tension in certain parts of my body and that I had never heard these powerful, present-focused mantras from anyone before. Quite the opposite, given a long history of trauma and hardships, I realized how incredibly cruel I had been to myself in my thoughts and negative self-talk. I committed to do the *fucking WERK* and heal my shit properly so I could do the same for others. If I can do it, you can too.

I have carefully crafted several mantras at the end of each chapter, which have been optimized in alignment for the highest good for all when used. I highly encourage you to try them out, rewrite them, or even create your own from these mantras as launch pads. This is the beginning of unlocking the portals to discovering your self-healing superpowers and redirecting you back to your innate power and wisdom. You are now attracting wonderful, healing, and mystical experiences into your life— you are creating your healing vortex within as you read this now. Pause for a minute and let yourself be present—with yourself … then keep on reading when you're ready to activate your inner vortex even more.

Have you noticed how many people are waking up right now? This mass awakening has been causing a huge rise in the portal and vortex activity in the earth's energy field and grid. Every time we set an intention, we open an energy portal, and new energy flows in. This creates a vortex, and energy starts to move. Old energy starts to flow out, creating space for new energy to flow in. This process is happening for everyone on earth, and it is creating a very intense time on our planet that many of us have been feeling even before the shock of 2020.

"Inner-standing" and "over-standing" the concepts of portals, vortices, and energy shifts are the keys to unlocking powerful healing and awakening within each of us and throughout the collective. As a side note, I prefer to use the words *inner-standing* and *over-standing* because the word *understanding* implies that you are under or beneath the concept of knowledge or information. When we "inner-stand" something, we truly take the information (information = light) inside our minds, bodies, and spirits; we create a close, private relationship and parallel frequency with the information inside our souls. When we "over-stand" something, we have completed or moved across an intervening space of information; we create a dynamic beyond the top or upper surface of information. Minor adjustments to the use of language in this way are controversial to some; however, I have found that they enhance our ability to trust ourselves and work with information in more collaborative ways and become skillful in self-mastery. Now let's go back to portals and vortices.

What Is a Portal? What Is a Vortex? How Do They Work Together?

A portal is an energetic opening, like a door. Every time we set an intention or decide to make a change—even to only a thought or mindset—we open an energy portal, and new energy comes into our lives, to our world, and to our entire being. When we open a portal with intentions of the highest good for ourselves and others, we then create a healing and awakening vortex. A vortex is like a tornado with two different swirling energies—one of the current or old energy and one of the new energy we wish to embrace. We create this vortex of energy that allows the old to disintegrate or spin off to make way for new energy to flow in. We are opening a portal where there once was a closed system, a closed mind, a fixed problem so we can tap into an open, flowing portal of positive change energy.

This process of change, healing, and awakening isn't always as smooth as we would like. This undoubtedly can create chaos just like an actual tornado or hurricane. Things that no longer serve us start to spin off into the cosmos, and we are forced to let go or reevaluate our inner and outer worlds. While this process can be initially chaotic or challenging, allowing this energy to move through intentionally is needed to break down barriers and become better versions of ourselves. We start to look at things in a different way and get unstuck from a fixed, closed system or "reality." *The portal is the doorway of intentions, and the vortex is the power and process of transformation.*

Much like a revolving door people go in and out of, a portal allows energy to move in and out of our lives. Old energy, limiting thoughts or beliefs, trapped emotions, and even tangible things come in and out of our lives and create this vast healing and awakening vortex of energy. Notice how many people are doing powerfully deep healing and awakening work right now. I can literally feel this surge of energy in the earth when I walk outside in my backyard and anchor my bare feet to the ground. I feel surges of intense grief, anger, shock, disbelief, sadness, transformation, energy release, joy, excitement, deep healing, and awakening on all levels; and it is beautiful to experience these emotions as a clairsentient—try it sometime to experience what I mean. This mass healing and awakening have a pulse that beats louder and stronger every mutha-loving day. Inner-standing how energy flows in and out of our lives and how we are impacted by the energy movements everyone is creating now is key to both individual and collective healing.

We are in the middle of a storm of new portals and energy vortices. Setting clear and aligned intentions for ourselves for our highest good and the greater good of humanity is so incredibly important right now. We don't want to get sucked into a vile vortex that harms us or that we didn't open with intention. We don't want to get trapped in that revolving door. We want to ensure the portals we open and the vortices we choose to travel through are free flowing and energy congruent with our healing and awakening intentions. When we do this, we can enhance our quality of life, create a flow of higher energetic frequencies, and explore ways to expand our consciousness within and around us.

Why Forty-Four Portals?

The number forty-four has always represented many important things to me. The initials in my name HH are forty-four in numerical form and in pager code (yes, I'm that old). It is also my favorite number of all time. Seeing the number forty-four ignites something special within me, a portal or pathway back to my soul and a reminder of how powerful I can be when I listen to my intuition. The more I have learned about healing and spirituality over the years, the more I have seen the number forty-four appear as a sign, a confirmation, and a clear message from the energies beyond our dimension that I am tapped into the healing vortex within my soul.

Just like every other number, forty-four has some interesting facts tied to it. The number forty-four in traditional numerology was the number of structure. It became the number of business, planning, and building strong foundations. In many realms of spirituality, the number forty-four is associated with an angel number and with higher states of consciousness. Angel numbers or alien numbers or just plain ole "numbers I dig" help us inner-stand complicated situations in our lives, whether you believe in angels, aliens, numbers, or *not*. They represent cosmic energy that has been sent to us by a higher force. When we find ourselves in hard life situations, these numbers come to us and remind us that every situation in life has a valuable lesson behind it.

The number forty-four is a representation of positive energy in your life. This is an important number to see, especially if you are going through hard life situations. Maybe that's why it keeps popping up for me so often. I used to believe life had to be hard, so I thought the same about healing myself. When I trusted that the universe always had my back, I could allow myself to surrender and heal, and easily and naturally shift my frequency higher.

The number forty-four is also a symbol of divine power and protection. When it shows up, I know everything I have started in life will be protected. Every project and responsibility will be surrounded by positive energy, and nothing will be able to stand in my way when I see my number forty-four. When we know we are being guided and protected, we can relax and fulfill the priorities in our lives without worrying about the outcome.

The number forty-four is also the traditional number of cards in oracle decks. The number forty-four is a symbol of passion as well. It helps you evoke the passions you forgot about along the way. For me that was writing. I had long ago given up the dream of being a writer, but the number forty-four showed me that following this passion was a pivotal part of my personal and professional growth. When we love something, nothing is hard to do, and people who are in love with their jobs create space to excel and achieve fulfillment in life. The number forty-four is like my own personal Tony Robbins, motivating me and coaching me to think positively and help myself get back in alignment.

The Pleiades Star Cluster, located above the Taurus constellation, is 444 light-years away from earth. The number 444 is considered a master healer number. The Pleiades is also my triple OG star home, and I will be returning there after I fulfill my soul's mission here on earth. Messier 44, also known as M44 or the Beehive Cluster, is an open star cluster in the constellation of Cancer; this star cluster also coincides with the Hyades near Aldebaran, Royal Fixed Star or "The Bulls Eye" in the Taurus constellation. Taurus Sun, Mercury, and Mars here. There is even a galaxy called Dragonfly 44; it is said to be the Milky Way Galaxy's "dark twin" because it consists of 99.99 percent dark matter. This is further evidence of how powerful just 0.01 percent of light or matter can be *and* more mystical, wacky, weird inspiration linked with the number forty-four.

The more I learned about the number forty-four, the more I knew that had to be the number of healing tools I included in this book. I also knew it would be a fierce reminder to return to the frequency of love every time my confidence dipped or I feared being too exposed, every time I hesitated to speak my truth and share my knowledge, and every time I procrastinated (a lot) or had a creative block. The number forty-four would appear as a magical mathematical code from the cosmos. Thanks to the number forty-four!

While finishing this book, I had yet another magical experience with the number forty-four while purchasing a very special Lemurian crystal for my birthday on May 4, 2021. For my "May the fourth be with you" solar return—or, as I prefer to call it, "May the quartz be with you"—birthday. I gifted myself a fabulous Lemurian seed crystal, which called my name (literally) at one of my favorite crystal shops in Mount Shasta, California. This beautiful Lemurian crystal made my solar return a very special day indeed. Lemurian crystals are encoded with information and lost secret wisdom put in these sacred stones before the destruction of the lost continent of Lemuria over twelve thousand years ago along with the lost land of Atlantis—but that topic is so vast that we will cover it in another book, maybe even four more to cover it properly.

When I brought my new Lemurian rock homey up to the register to check out, I totally hit it off with the woman working there, and we started talking cosmic crystal people talk. She then asked whether I wanted a reading on the Lemurian crystal and that they offered them only for the Lemurians. "But of course," I said and proceeded to watch as she pulled out a manual and started carefully looking over every inch of my new crystal friend. She came back with several handouts and information on crystal personalities and declared that the Lemurian crystal I had picked out carried an energy frequency of the number forty-four! That Lemurian crystal probably *was* mine some fifty thousand years ago during my lives in Lemuria as the master crystal librarian. Now all I had to do was work with my crystal homey and activate it again. There are no such things as coincidences. Once you realize that, you will start to understand how incredibly powerful you truly are. I could go on and on about the cosmic significance of the number forty-four and how it relates to hundreds of areas of my life on earth and in the stars, but I think you get the point. Now let me talk about energy healing, since it is a huge component of this book.

What Is Energy Healing?

Everything is energy healing. That's right. Because everything is energy, we can say that every healing modality is technically an energy healing modality. What are your thoughts and behaviors if not energy? Your words, emotions, consciousness, and body are all different constellations of energy moving at different frequencies and speeds. Energy healing is a holistic or "whole person" approach to healing that acts on the mind, body, and spirit. The types of energy healing modalities that exist are far too nebulous in their infinitude to list here. You will get firsthand experience with many types of energy healing throughout this book. I will also guide you through these energy portals and how to use various energy healing techniques for self-healing and self-awakening.

For over seventeen years, I have studied, practiced, and taught about the subject of healing and energy psychology, trauma and addiction recovery, empaths and starseeds, altered states of consciousness, existential and spiritual awakenings, meditation, astrology, breathwork, tantra, and, most importantly, how to inner-stand your personal energy to enhance the innate healing and awakening capacity we all possess. My audiences connect with my practical, straightforward, down-to-earth approach and often experience deep healing, realizations, awakenings, and can reclaim their personal power in the world by activating their unique self-healing superpowers. Many of my clients identify as indigo, crystal, or rainbow children; light workers; empaths; highly sensitive persons; intuitives; and/ or starseeds. Many of my clients come to me and have no idea what any of those labels mean but soon discover they very much identify as one of the above-listed souls. Let me explain briefly what each means. And, yes, you can identify as more than one or all of them!

Indigo, Crystal, and Rainbow Children

Individuals from these three soul groups often possess special or supernatural abilities, including telepathy, clairvoyance, intuitive energy reading, deep empathy, and reality shifting. Indigos are infused with the power of advocacy. They are "rebels with a cause" and can fight intensely when they see unfairness in the world. Crystals are infused with the light, joy, and clarity of the quartz master healing crystals for which they are named. They feel deeply and tend to be more fair and kind than their indigo and rainbow siblings. Often diagnosed with some form of autism, Rainbow Children are the latest wave of healing souls to come to Earth. They are here to help humanity during this difficult time in our collective evolution. I go into greater detail on these three groups later in the book.

Light Workers

Light Workers are special souls from a variety of planets and realms who have agreed to incarnate to help Earth and other worlds evolve. They up-level humanity and raise the consciousness of everyone around them by shining light on the dark corners of the world. Their primary purpose is to spread kindness, goodness, and love to every living being they meet. Light workers are not beholden to any planet, culture, society, or mission. There are many different types of Light Workers including: grid workers, timeline workers, frequency healers, seers, divine blueprint holders, astral travelers, messengers, the way showers, unifiers, and ascension guides. Many Indigos, Crystals, and Rainbow Children identify as light workers as well.

Empaths

Empaths are people who are highly attuned to the feelings, emotions, thoughts, and sensations of those around them. Their ability to discern what others are feeling goes beyond empathy and extends to taking those feelings on; feeling what another person is feeling at a deep emotional and sensory level. Empaths appear to have more mirror neurons in the brain than others, suggesting a neurological basis for inner-standing this phenomenon. Many empaths have extrasensory or psychic gifts that can be overwhelming to them until they learn how to use these gifts as tools for healing and awakening in safe and healthy ways. There are a wide variety of different types of empaths, each of which has a unique set of superpowers. Different types of empaths include: emotional empaths, cognitive empaths, intuitive empaths, physical empaths, psychometric empaths, earth empaths, animal empaths, plant empaths, dream empaths, and psychic empaths. All empaths are highly sensitive persons (HSPs), but not all HSPs are empaths.

Highly Sensitive Persons (HSPs)

These individuals have a distinct personality trait that affects as many as one out of every five people who have a sensitive nervous system. They are aware of subtleties in their surroundings and heightened sensitivity to, and distress caused by, certain people, places, and things (like foods and fragrances). HSPs are more easily overwhelmed when in a highly stimulating environment and may even experience trauma-level reactions to sensitivities.

Intuitives

An intuitive person is someone who senses things about people and their surroundings and their experiences that aren't so evident to more "normal" people. When their intuition is strong, we may call them "psychic," "clairvoyant" (sees things or has visions), "clairaudient" (hears things or channels), "claircognizant" (knows things or is insightful), "clairsentient" (feels things, senses, or is intuitive), or "clairgustant" (smells or tastes things for intuitive downloads).

Starseeds

Starseeds are individuals who originated from far-distant stars and solar systems, planets, and galaxies. These highly evolved souls carry a plethora of wisdom and special abilities that hibernate deep within the core of their being. All starseeds are encoded with activation encryptions that will unlock their knowledge and talents at a predetermined or spontaneous time on earth, for the retrieval of this information is to be utilized for very specific purposes. Most starseeds feel a sense of misplacement, like they were aliens dropped here on earth without a compass, so they harbor a sense of emptiness and longing to find or go back to their "true home." I also highly encourage us to think of the starseed types as archetypes or "starchetypes" on the healing and awakening journey that anyone can tap into for support regardless of what star home you may or may not identify with.

All You Other Beautiful Souls

Even if you don't identify with any of these groups or categories, the portals and vortices in this book will help you on your journey to heal anything if you so choose. This book will also help you gain valuable and easy-to-apply tools for accessing your healing vortex within and unlocking the code to your unique self-healing superpowers. After all, labels can be overrated, and I empower each of you reading this to create your own unique soul name or identity that resonates for you.

THE HEALING VORTEX WITHIN: FORTY-FOUR PORTALS TO AWAKEN YOUR SELF-HEALING SUPERPOWERS

CHAPTER 1

Be Open to Entering the First Healing Portal

Healing is an inside job.
—B. J. Palmer

No soul gets out of this life (and thousands of past lives, for you old souls) without experiencing something from which healing is needed—whether it is physical, mental, emotional, spiritual, energetic, relational, or a mix of all these elements. Most of us can agree that after surviving the year 2020, we have experienced painful realizations, transformations, and awakenings, and we are personally and collectively in need of healing, especially for our souls.

But what is healing? The meaning of healing is broad and complex: To heal = to restore to health or soundness. To restore to spiritual wholeness. To return to optimal health. In psychology, healing involves reordering a person's sense of purpose in the universe or the process of evolving one's personality toward greater and more complex wholeness. Healing can also be thought of as the process of bringing together aspects of one's self, body-mind-spirit, at deeper levels of inner knowing, leading towards integration and balance with each aspect having equal importance and value.

The word *heal* is from the root word *hal*, which means "holy" or "spiritually pure." In this we can see that healing is a spiritual word at its core. Which brings me to my opinion on healing: true healing involves reconnecting with your soul, rediscovering your soul's voice (intuition), and entering the healing vortex within your soul. Cool. Sounds great. "How the fuck do I do that though?" you might ask. Great question. I am going to walk you through just that.

First, we need to understand that surface-level healing equates to surface-level results. We live in a society that has become consumed with appearances and quick fixes. The longest journey you will ever take is the one from your mind to your soul. If we want to heal on the soul level, at the core of the wound, we must be open to healing. And being open to healing means going within that very first portal or gateway. No one else can do it for you. Healing and awakening are inside jobs "fo' realz."

No matter how long ago I began my healing journey and awakening process, there is still plenty to work on and more than enough that needs to be healed. The challenge for me and for everyone else is to be open to healing, to be open to this process. Now what exactly does that mean? This is the first step in truly healing anything: be open to healing. When I say "open," I mean you must commit to starting this work yourself rather than giving your power to heal or awaken away to any external person, place, or thing. The portals you will be taking to find that sacred vortex within your soul are *your* inner portals.

I often remind my clients that they are the ones in charge of their healing journeys. They are the pilots navigating their healing and awakening journeys; I am simply the copilot. That's right—you are in charge, and you decide where you go, when you go, how long you stay, and what you want to do at each portal along the way. I also find it incredibly important to remind my clients that they are the experts on them. No one knows you better than you. No one can do the work for you.

I remember telling this to a very resistant client. She said to me with a big sigh, "Can't you just wave a magic wand or something and make me better? I don't want to do all this work. I mean, you're the doctor." It took everything in me not to laugh, because she was dead serious. I'd much rather teach my clients how to activate their own magic wands, but many people don't want to take full personal accountability for their innate magic *or* their healing and awakening journey. You can't outsource your healing and awakening, not even in the day and age of technology. The sad reality is that everyone is looking for a quick fix nowadays, and that prolongs and sometimes prevents real healing and meaningful personal growth.

You must allow healing into your energy field and into your mind, body, heart, and soul. Traveling through these healing portals and entering the healing vortex within mean you are in control of your healing and awakening journey. It means taking your power back. It means allowing that inner whirlpool of cosmic energy to form at your core. Your innate capacity to heal anything and everything is so much greater than you have been conditioned to believe. We are all born with this intrinsic self-healing and self-awakening ability; we just need to reconnect to it now. This is the first healing portal. Will you travel through it? The choice is yours.

Open yourself up to healing by opening your body posture. Take a long, slow, deep breath in through your nose and out through your mouth. Imagine a swirling, sparkling white or golden light entering through the top of your head and infusing your entire body with a luminous glow. This sparkling light fills up every cell in your body and swirls down and out through the bottom of your feet. Continue to visualize this light as you say these healing-vortex-within mantras:

> "I release all blocks and fears to self-healing now."
> "I am choosing to enter the first healing portal now."
> "My mind, body, and spirit are open to healing now."

CHAPTER 2

The Portal of Belief

Believe you can and you're halfway there.
—Theodore Roosevelt

Believing you can heal helps you align your energy to take positive action. The person who wishes to be healed must be willing to do some of the work. Most people just want a healer to heal them without effort on their part. However, in my experience, the healer can bring about only a temporary cure at best.

There have been many clients I have worked with over the years who were simply not ready to heal. I have had even more clients who doubted their ability to heal and struggled to believe in their healing process and the power of the healing journey—not just the desired outcome of feeling better. Deep healing work isn't a magic pill your doctor prescribes; it requires you to do the "werk" and stay in an energetic state of believing you can heal (at least most of the time—perfection not required here). And I do mean *werk*. The word "work", spelled basic bitch style, is a matrix word that is coded with resistance frequencies, and it triggers the idea of slavery in the human vessel. Notice how your body reacts to the word "work" when you say it aloud. Now in your best drag queen voice say the word *"werk"* and notice the difference. You will see me use *"werk"* to activate playful frequencies, to make healing and awakening fun again, and to create results even faster. It can take approximately 400 repetitions to create a new synapse in the brain, unless it is done in play, in which case it only takes 10-20 repetitions. So you better *werk* those mantras, believe in the healing power of play and believe in your ability to heal too!

Your belief in your body's ability to heal itself directly influences the result you experience. Leverage the placebo effect to your advantage. If you believe you're getting better using whatever remedies you've decided on, your belief will manifest and make it so. If you buy into any diagnosis that what you're experiencing is "incurable" or "chronic," this will be your experience. Do whatever you need to do to stay focused on your complete and total healing. Concentrate on releasing doubt and fear and returning to feeling, knowing, and believing you are healthy and well. If you believe it will work and stick with it, you can heal yourself.

There have been too many times to count in my life when I felt broken and incapable of letting go, forgiving, and truly believing in the power of self-healing. After a particularly horrifying sexual assault in college, I felt too fragmented to try to heal. So I buried it, locked it away, and numbed the "f" out. It worked, too, for about ten years, until it all came flooding back when I started working with trauma survivors again during my pre- and postdoc internship years at UCSF. One day a week, each intern had an on-call shift for the rape treatment center at the main hospital, and my very first shift alone brought my trauma right back up to the surface. It triggered the worst feelings of panic, loss, and violation a human can endure. But under the triggers is where true healing happens. With the support of my inner circle and a variety of gifted healers, I started to believe I could heal and travel through the portal of belief. This is a pivotal and powerful portal on the healing journey that cannot be overlooked for deeper and complete healing to occur.

It's one thing to open yourself up to healing, but it is a whole other endeavor to believe you can and will heal. It is very normal to have doubts about our abilities to heal at times, especially when it comes to trauma, heartbreak, grief, and loss. I want to encourage you to find at least some part of you that believes you can heal. Allow that part of you to grow each day. As your belief that you can heal grows, you will heal in ways you never thought imaginable. Even if only 1 percent of you believes it, that is a great place to start. Build up to 51 percent over time, and then you got that majority-rules vibe. You don't need to believe in yourself 100 percent or all the time, but you need to do so at least enough so you can leap through the portal of belief. It is about progress here, *not perfection*. No one believes at the 100 percent level 100 percent of the time, and that's okay. I know that part of you already believes you can heal; otherwise, you wouldn't be reading this book right now.

Close your eyes, connect to your breath, and visualize what it will look like and feel like once you have overcome your current struggles. Think about how good it will feel to fully own your personal power in the world. Practice saying these healing-vortex-within mantras now:

"I believe I can heal and awaken myself."
"I am increasing my ability to heal more and more every day."
"I am choosing to believe in my ability to heal now."

CHAPTER 3

The Portal of Healing and Awakening

Psychology is incomplete without spirituality.
—Stan Grof

Stan Grof is one of the few people in the field of psychology whom I genuinely respect and admire. He is the godfather of transpersonal psychology (or spiritual psychology) and created the "holotropic breathwork method," which has helped me heal and awaken more than any other type of therapy that exists to date. BreathWERK makes my soul TWERK (but more on that later). The word *transpersonal* is defined as "experiences in which the sense of identity or self extends beyond (trans) the individual or personal to encompass wider aspects of humankind, life, psyche, or the cosmos." Transpersonal psychology focuses on healing and awakening and developing beyond the conventional or individual levels; it taps you into universal or cosmic consciousness.

Spirituality and energy are often considered dirty words in many pockets of Western medicine, psychology, psychiatry, and other conservative sects that believe in the "treat the symptoms" approach and that only medicine and "scientific" methods are real. Treating the symptoms doesn't cure anything. In fact, it can often create other problems including dependence on expensive and toxic medications. Healing on the surface is just that—superficial. Deep, meaningful, and sustainable healing involves going much deeper and inner-standing the root cause, the energy systems around this, and believing there is value in the unseen. Many people have a hard time with this concept and will remain miserable for too long as a result.

You don't need to believe in something to be affected by it. Many of us don't believe in taxes, but they sure do affect us.

I believe energy is the only thing that is real, *and* everything is energy. I am a specialized type of psychologist with a long background in various forms of energy healing. Energy psychology encompasses a beautiful blend of methods designed to improve physical, mental, emotional, and spiritual well-being. Common methods used in energy psychology are Emotional Freedom Technique (EFT) or tapping, creative healing methods, and other holistic or integrative approaches.

Energy psychology or anything involving these more Eastern medicine concepts wasn't used at all in my graduate training. More conservative, old-school psychologists frowned on these methods. I have found these methods to be the most helpful in healing numerous ailments for myself and my clients time and time again, and I believe strongly in the power of energy healing. Combining Eastern and Western healing modalities further enhances our ability to heal and awaken.

I became particularly interested in energy healing and working with the charkas in 2013 when dealing with a series of miserable health issues that Western medicine was only making worse. I remember reading the book *The Wheels of Life, The Classic Guide to the Chakra System* by Anodea Judith, PhD. My mom saw the book one day when she came to visit and said, "Oh I love that book. I read it when I was pregnant with you!" *Wow*, I thought, since I had been magnetically drawn to it, and it felt so incredibly meaningful and familiar to me. This was the beginning of my healing, and awakening journey and synchronicities like that kept appearing.

Healing is the process of transforming a hurt person or an unaligned person into a blissful, aligned person. The disorder we see outside in our lives is simply because there is disorder inside us. We are hurt and are suffering. But hurt is a vibrational frequency (a specific energy), and healing is another vibrational frequency. The hurt vibration creates disorder, while the healing vibration creates order. The journey from hurt to healing is the awakening. This is something I wish I had been taught or somehow addressed in my doctorate program or any of traditional and "well-renowned" mental health training I slogged through for many painful years to earn my degree and license. Most schools provide indoctrination, not real education. It is so important to question what we are taught and tap into each of our unique and sovereign truths on healing and awakening.

Healing is awakening, and awakening is healing. The two are synonymous in my opinion because everything is connected. The philosophy of unity consciousness is that all life is one (one Source, one consciousness, one divinity), temporarily expressing itself in this third-dimensional form. But because we have lost the awareness of our connection to all things, our basic experience of life has become one of separation. We experience ourselves as beings that are essentially separate from everything else in creation and separate from the universal Source of creation or "God." I know the "God" word makes people all kinds of uncomfortable, so feel free to use whatever resonates best with you. Some other suggestions are: Source, The Universe, and The Robot Alien Overlords that run this wacky simulation. The choice is yours. What is most important here is to realize we have been conditioned by our egos to believe we are all separate.

This creates all kinds of issues and false identities, which over time imprint and condition every level of our human system—our bodies, minds, emotions, and even sense of spirituality. The web of this separation conditioning and polarizing distortions is incredibly pervasive, unimaginably deep, existing on multidimensional levels, and it completely distorts our experience of being human. In addition to creating a myriad of emotional issues, it also creates blockages in our human energy system.

So often I begin working with clients who believe they're depressed and anxious, and have self-diagnosed themselves as "bad" or "sick" or "stuck." This is because the process of healing and awakening often begins with a "dark night of the soul" or, in other words, an earth-shattering existential crisis. Furthermore, both healing and awakening don't come in pretty, little packages scheduled under your control. They often come at the least expected time and in the most gut-wrenching way to fully get our attention and force us out of our complacent bubble of detachment.

The universe has shaken us to awaken us. That couldn't be more true than of the years of 2020 and 2021. We have all been through unimaginable pain, trauma, loss, and personal and collective intense energetic surges on both ends of the spectrum of light/highs and polarizing/lows. So many of us have been personally and collectively shaken to our cores on all levels.

More and more people are waking up, going inward, tapping into those portals, and activating forgotten soul vortices of self-healing superpowers.

We are realizing that change is necessary if we want to live healthier, happier lives and improve the state of the world. People now more than ever are open to healing (chapter 1) and believe they can heal (chapter 2). Change starts within, and if you can change your energy (thoughts, emotions, behaviors, and so forth), you change your entire life. The ripple effect of this is undeniable and truly creates a wave of love and positive energy that crashes on the shores of even the most remote islands. The portal of healing and awakening is within you. Are you ready to activate it now?

Healing *is* awakening, and awakening *is* healing. The more you heal and release, the more you awaken the fire within you. The more you ignite that fire, the more you will see other aspects that lovingly need healing attention. The journey is a continuous spiral to deeper and deeper layers of self or higher and higher dimensional realms of consciousness. Allow this process to unfold organically since we are all works of art in progress until the day we die. Spend some time connecting to these healing-vortex-within mantras and say them aloud (and create your own that resonate with you):

> "I am healing and awakening myself more every day."
> "I am open to seeing hardships as opportunities to heal
> and grow."
> "I choose to heal and awaken myself."

CHAPTER 4

The Art of Portaling

Art should comfort the disturbed and disturb the comfortable.
—Caesar A. Cruz

One of my favorite artists is a man named Pricasso. He paints Picassoesque masterpieces with his penis, scrotum, and buttocks. Now that's my kind of art! His paintings are true master*pieces* painted completely with his "piece," his favorite "tool," naked as the day he was born while wearing nothing but a giant, hot-pink foam cowboy hat, matching bowtie, and a charming Aussie smile. This kind of fearless, deeply authentic, erotic self-expression takes *balls*. LOL. All penis jokes aside, this gorgeous one-of-a-kind soul is a magical mirror for us all, reflecting to us how deeply joyful and creative we can be when we are comfortable with our bodies, expressing authenticity and vulnerability. Now that's great art!

"Art should comfort the disturbed and disturb the comfortable" is a quote many artists hold very dear. What happens when we get too comfortable? We become complacent, stagnant, and miserable. Real personal growth begins outside the comfort zone. Leave the comfort zone? *I don't know about all that,* you might be thinking. Don't let yourself equate the unknown with bad. Many people get caught in the trap that healing or therapy or this awakening spirituality mumbo jumbo must not be for them because they are simply afraid of the unknown, afraid of change; and the sad reality is that many people will die without ever trying a single mantra. How silly is that, dude?

If you're someone who would prefer to stay miserable and complain about all the ways your life isn't the masterpiece of art you would like it to be or had envisioned for yourself while also refusing to take any small step to change it, then you might need to spend some extra time with the first three chapters. Some of us need more time than others to dive into the artful portals of healing and awakening. But don't worry. None of the mantras or activities in this book involve painting anything with your penis or any other body parts. I mean, who could top Pricasso anyways?

The greatest masterpiece of art we will ever create is the art of portaling along our healing and awakening journey. What kind of art do you want to create? What type of universe or parallel reality do you want to choose to create now? Think about it for a minute. What do you like to do that is creative? How can you apply that creative outlet or passion to healing? Remember: you create the portals, and you decide when, where, and how you glide or stride through them. We all need a creative, artistic outlet of some kind, even if we don't think we're good at it.

Here are some things I like to do creatively that might help inspire your unique creative portaling process and activate the healing vortex within:

- Creatively clean or reorganize with color and music
- Dance
- Sing
- Give myself a fashion show
- Color a mandala or anything in an adult coloring book with giant profane words
- Garden
- Cook
- Write
- Make a fun, new playlist
- Pretend I'm one of my favorite musicians for a day
- Work with my tarot or oracle decks
- Make a new seasonal altar
- Find new poets and artists to support
- Play with my cats
- Invent a new way to heal I've never heard of
- Pick three books off my shelf, pick a random page number, and see what all three have in common (it's like an oracle or tarot reading with books)

- Make up new words and add them to the *Urban Dictionary* (you'd be surprised by how many of those slang words are mine)
- Pretend I'm an alien who speaks only with sounds or noises when at a store
- Find a new way to be creatively lazy and do nothing.

Should I keep going? That might need to be a whole other book, but you get the idea. Get the art of portaling creative juices flowing—*yas gawd*. Find a way to weave in some form of art or self-expression throughout your healing journey and make it yours. They don't call it the "healing arts" for nothing, ya dig? We are all works of art until the day we die. Do you want to be a blank canvas or a gorgeous, colorful tapestry of a life well lived? Practice say these healing-vortex-within mantras loudly and proudly to further activate the healing artist within now:

> "Life is art, and I am the artist of my life."
> "I engage in fun and creative outlets to support my healing
> and awakening journey."
> "I am choosing to see my journey in life as my greatest
> masterpiece."

CHAPTER 5

The Portal of Storytelling

Your biography becomes your biology.
—Caroline Myss

Oh, the stories we tell ourselves! We all have those stories we tell that are uplifting, funny, sentimental, and in alignment with love. Then we all have those stories that paint a picture of us as victims, losers, failures, or grotesque, monster villains. We can simply reference the multibillion-dollar industry that is entertainment and see how incredibly captivating and profitable all kinds of stories can be. The stories we tell ourselves about ourselves, our relationships, and the world literally become energy that is then encoded in our very biological makeup.

Think about the different kinds of energy you experience when you watch a romantic movie, action movie, or drama. There is a very real, energetic component of all stories, especially emotional energy. Within your energy field exists emotional energy, which is created by your internal and external experiences in life related to past or present relationships, traumatic experiences or memories, beliefs, attitudes, and habits. Your emotions reside in your physical body and then interact with your cells, subsequently forming an energy portal within that carries information that is both symbolic and literal. Your body contains your history, and every thought or story you experience travels through your biological system. In this sense, your biography becomes your biology. The stories you tell yourself and others are powerful portals that constantly create your reality, mood, self-talk, and sense of self.

Healing is a very active and internal process that involves examining one's attitudes, beliefs, thoughts, feelings, energetic states, and relationships, relating them to the stories we tell ourselves and others. Healing often involves rewriting the unhelpful narratives that keep us sick and miserable. Healing involves investigating the ways we have taken on archetypal roles such as the victim (blames others or gives power to others), the saboteur (destroys rather than deals with challenges), the child (lacks accountability and responsibility), and the prostitute (compromises self, lacks boundaries, says yes when they mean no—not literal hookers).

There are many other archetypal roles or characters we can play in the stories we tell, many of which are far more accurate and empowering. They include the hero, the dreamer, the entrepreneur, the lover, the philanthropist, the healer, the mystic, the starseed, and the list goes on. Take a look at the stories you tell yourself and what they say about you and find any helpful insights into the areas where you may need healing. What story are you choosing to tell about your life? What kind of story are you creating every day with your thoughts, feelings, words, and energy? What kind of story do you want to create?

Here is an example from my brain womb regarding the power of storytelling and the realness of the struggle in trying to write this damn book for three years. This is from my private journal, dated December 1, 2020:

It twas the best of times, it twas the worst of times. Why do I fucking hate Christmas so much? Oh, yeah trauma and family drama. Ho, Ho, Ho … will I ever be done healing and awakening or what dude? Reflecting on the intense weekend of inner work, shifting and collapsing and merging timelines. Reflecting on all I've survived this past year alone, laying on my biomat, listening to some sound healing frequencies, feeling overwhelmed with the deepest sense of gratitude. Also, feeling that paradoxical pull between worlds of healing and awakening, awakening and healing when a voice says to me … "they're the same thing beyotch, DUH." Uhhh, thank you higher self or past life drag queen self … or both? Both fasho. I feel like I am teetering dangerously on a mental balance beam between two worlds, two opposing teams in my brain. On one side "why is this damn book not finished bitch … goat noise, goat noise, crash," vs on the other side, "you got this, you be writing this book badabing badaboom like every day in your head, just learn to type as fast as you think immediately if not soon k thanks." I'm terrified of falling off this mental balance beam, afraid to fail, afraid to succeed, not even wanting to move forward or choose a side to fall into the dismal abyss of despair or the arms of … why choose a side, I'm Switzerland bitch (minus the creepy CERN stuff), even though it has taken me three plus years to write this book, I'm not rooting for either side here. Then out of the sky I see a glorious magical Unicorn-Pegasus rainbow glittery hybrid GAWDASS, but not flying, she's driving the Mary Kay, HAÚTE pink Cadillac of Alien STARSEED UFOs and hovers over me sending down a luminescent, rainbow channel of light completely enveloping my entire body and auric field. Next a rickety rope ladder is dropped down ushering me to climb in. "Can't you beam me up?" I ask, as the unicorn UFO chauffer looks down at me, "girl it's your daydream brain dream visualization thingy, you gotta climb, HUNTEE!" And just like that I shimmy up the rope ladder and am whisked away to the magical land of Unicorns where books are no longer hard to write, yay!

See how that works? I could've kept telling myself, "OMG. Books are so hard to write. What a loser you are for it taking so long. I mean, it's not like your life and the whole world have been turned upside down and changed like four dozen times drastically in the last few years or anything." Damn, that inner critic can be harsh. Or … I could create a better, improved narrative in which the book gets done magically. And I'm telling you that unicorn is a constant reference point for me when I need to remind myself of how powerful the stories we tell ourselves truly are. Practice using these healing-vortex-within mantras to empower yourself around the stories you tell and be the ultimate narrator and creator of your life:

> "I choose to release old narratives and tell my story from the frequency of love and gratitude."
> "I am rewriting my narrative to deeply heal and become the best version of myself."
> "Stories are powerful portals that I create consciously for the highest good of all."

CHAPTER 6

Denial—Not Just a Portal in Egypt

What you ignore and deny, you delay; what
you accept and face, you conquer.
—Robert Tew

Most people know that the first step to healing anything is acknowledging there is something present that needs healing. You cannot heal something you don't acknowledge. Yet all too often, people deny the reality of the problem. They refuse to believe it exists and therefore resist that they may require any form of healing whatsoever. Denial negates certain realities from your conscious awareness as a form of self-protection for you to cope with life. You block out the realities you believe you cannot handle and hide them in your unconscious.

Denying realities causes greater inner conflict as you operate your life on two levels of awareness, one based on the denial while the other on the level of accepting what is. Because you deny something, that doesn't cause it to disappear. Actually, quite the opposite will happen. It is in your energy, and you will create experiences until it is resolved; it will eat away at you until you stop denying. It will seep into all other areas of your life until it eventually explodes. Would you rather deal with detonating a small grenade-size bomb or a nuclear weapon the size of Texas? The choice is yours and how courageously you embark on the healing journey within and identify exactly what it is you need and want to heal.

All illness is a form of denial since it is created by resisting learning the lesson from your life experiences. You can learn a lot from your mistakes when you aren't busy denying them. Suppressing the experience into your unconscious is a form of denial. "Denial ain't just a river in Egypt" (thank you,

Mark Twain). Let's get real familiar with that classic defense mechanism of denial so we can kick it to the curb. Classic forms of denial behavior include:

1. Hiding from the world, being aloof (addictions, avoidance, or isolation). People with addictions often deny they have an issue and continue their addictive behavior. "I don't have a problem; I can quit anytime." We've all heard (or said) that one before.

2. Being busy so you don't focus on what has happened. For example, busily helping others to avoid looking at what has happened to you, or you just focus on being busy doing things without acknowledging how they have affected you.

3. Blaming others for your life situation or playing victim. People may push your buttons, but they didn't create them. You created your buttons by not resolving some inner conflicts. To blame is to "be lame"! You don't move through the healing process. Trust me, I know. Most of us have been there since it seems so much easier to point fingers than to look within, but this only creates more suffering and delays living a good life.

4. Having passive anger. What people are really angry about is that they aren't achieving their desired lifestyle because they are in denial. Anger is a message that you are out of alignment and/or have an unmet need you aren't clearly communicating.

Quite often people deny the grief they feel when they lose someone and try to carry on their lives by doing things so they can avoid feeling the perceived loss. However, denying the grief doesn't make it go away; it is still in the person's energy and will be there until it is resolved by creating other experiences of perceived loss. We know what we resist persists, and we sometimes may require a bigger wake-up call or cosmic smackdown of pain before we are ready to look at it. Pain is often a great motivator to initiate healing. If we don't feel physical, mental, emotional, or spiritual pain because of a lack of awareness, we will create perceived drama in life to get us to look at why we are creating such experiences and finally resolve our inner conflicts. Remember: our souls want to heal and awaken; the universe wants us to heal and awaken. This is what we signed up for when our soul contracts were made for this lifetime.

So now comes the hard part. Get brutally honest and accountable with yourself about what you need to heal and why. First, let's travel through the denial portal to get out the other side by acknowledging any areas you may have been avoiding. Go on … do it! Staying in the middle of the denial portal is like being trapped in an elevator. Eventually, it's going to get real stank in there if you don't find a way out. Moving through the denial portal is about your responsibility to heal for you by you.

When you acknowledge that you have created the problem, illness, or challenge for a reason, you are ready to go through the healing process. You accept that you are currently in a low-energy vibration, reflecting there is unresolved energy inside you that needs and deserves to be transmuted. Healing begins when you choose to stop resisting and accept what is. Learn the life lesson and apply moving forward so you don't block your flow of energy or joy anymore.

Next, identify the root cause. With this step, I'm not talking about buying into any diagnosis about what you're experiencing; it is all too easy to say, "Well, I'm depressed" or "I have chronic PTSD" or "I just like to yell" or "It just runs in our family." You are *not* your diagnosis. And even more importantly, you are not a prisoner of trauma, bad genes, or disease. These are all-too-common blocks to doing the inner work. These labels sometimes become barriers to healing at the core. But *why* are you depressed? But what caused the chronic PTSD? Where did you learn, "It is okay to yell at others"? While yelling may run in the family, where did it begin and why?

Take some time to go within to identify the core emotions, feelings, and actions that may have led to your feeling less than vibrant or getting thrown out of alignment for however long you have been struggling. Any problem, disease, or injury offers an opportunity to increase awareness. What is going on in your life that triggered this challenging state of being? Get honest with yourself as you review your choices leading up until now.

Your healing and awakening adventure is waiting for you to jump in and rev up the engine already. It's not all hard shit, I promise; a great deal of this inner work is feeling alive again and connected to your purpose in life. Think of how much better your life will be when these limitations are gone, gone, *gone*! Your healing vortex within wants the truth, the whole truth, and nothing but the truth, baby. But can you handle the truth?

Don't rush this step. I cannot emphasize that enough. Often we think we are being honest with ourselves and others, but denial isn't just a river in Egypt. Check your defenses. Check your blind spots and get support from a trusted friend, healer, therapist, family member, or coach. Or you may find it through journaling.

Take a moment to close your eyes and take three long, slow, deep breaths. Then come back to this page and ask yourself, "What do I need to heal and why?" Spend five to ten minutes writing your answer out. Don't overthink it; just be radically honest with yourself. Say these healing-vortex-within mantras as often as needed as an added boost:

> "I am fully accountable for my healing and awakening journey."
>
> "It is safe to look within at the root of my problems."
>
> "Being honest with myself *is* healing and awakening myself."

CHAPTER 7

The Portal of Self-Awareness

Your pain is an opportunity for you to learn about yourself.
—Gary Zukav

One of the most important elements of activating the self-healing and self-awakening vortex within is the portal of self-awareness and of continually getting to know yourself. I cannot overemphasize the importance of knowing yourself *and* knowing you will change along your journey. You must be willing to portal through self-awareness many times to recognize what is and isn't working in your life. You must be self-aware to become an even better version of yourself. You must want to learn about yourself and get to know yourself time and time again on this ever-changing journey.

Now, what does knowing yourself mean? To know yourself, you must go inward. Think about all the things that make you feel like you. The things you like or hate, the triggers that set you off, the ways you express yourself, soothe yourself, and show up in the world. Knowing ourselves, rediscovering ourselves, and having self-awareness aren't as easy as one might think.

Many people have a hard time with self-knowledge, and we can easily experience soul loss; existential crises; and mental, physical, and emotional symptoms that create a sense of detachment from the self. Please remember that these are normal parts of life, and you can always reconnect to yourself and better inner-stand who you are. I highly recommend starting with measures like the Myers-Briggs test, Enneagram, and/or your full astrology chart (or Starseed Galactic Origins Reading) if you don't know where to begin. The synergy between these measures when combined is quite powerful, and it is a method I often use with my clients. There are many other helpful ways to build a relationship with yourself.

There are hundreds of ways to connect more deeply with yourself. The thing about inner-standing the personality is that once you truly inner-stand it, you can transcend it—because you aren't your personality, astrology sign, enneagram number, what you do for work, where you live, what fancy letters you have or don't have behind your name, or a bunch of other dumb, arbitrary labels people think define them. You are a soul with a unique frequency, and figuring out what that energetic frequency is will be one of your greatest assets on this journey as a human on earth and *beyond*. What are a few words you would use to describe your unique frequency or the "energy of your soul" if you will?

List some. Go on. List at least three in your journal now. Come back and add to it regularly.

Place one hand on your heart and the other on your forehead and repeat these healing-vortex-within mantras aloud:

> "I connect to my personal power through self-knowledge and self-awareness."
> "Self-awareness gives me the capacity to learn from my mistakes and heal anything."
> "Inner-standing myself and being self-aware unlock my self-healing superpowers."

CHAPTER 8

The Portals of Problem-Solving

So what if you have a hunchback, honey? Throw
some glitter on it and go dancing!
—James St. James, Party Monster

We live in a culture obsessed with perfection, image, and presenting oneself in a favorable light. This fixation on perfection makes us sicker and sicker. It's inauthentic and unobtainable. We create more problems for ourselves when we avoid our weaknesses. When you embrace your flaws, you release yourself from the need to be perfect, and you heal yourself. Let's be honest: whether we want to admit it or not, there are many things in life we aren't good at doing. Even so, it's not easy to embrace your weaknesses and accept the fact that there are some things you aren't good at. Several things can make it difficult to recognize your weaknesses. Excessive pride, low self-esteem, or fears that you're fundamentally not good enough can get in the way. On the other hand, you might genuinely believe you're good at a particular thing until the truth punches you upside the head—metaphorically speaking, of course.

Often when we enter the healing vortex, we feel more vulnerable than usual, and this can translate to an inner sense of "I'm weak." Embracing our weakness is healing, but it's even more important to allow deeper levels of healing to occur. I would like to share the amazing things that can happen when you decide to fully embrace your weaknesses. Fully embracing your weaknesses is the only way to work on them. Doing so allows you to make positive changes in your life and creates growth opportunities. Will you make peace with your weaknesses or work to only conceal them? Regardless of your choice, fully acknowledging them is the first step.

Working on your weaknesses can yield amazing results and solve numerous problems. For instance, low self-confidence might be hindering your ability to attain success and happiness. In this case, focusing on that weakness and taking full responsibility for it would produce several positive changes. It would likely unveil hidden potential and create significant momentum in your life. Of course, trying to get rid of a certain weakness isn't always the best idea. Not every weakness can or should be changed. Sometimes all you need is the courage to recognize it and accept that you can't or shouldn't do anything about it. You can always throw some glitter on that weakness or perceived flaw as you boldly own it. After all, imperfections are part of being human.

Fears can masquerade as weaknesses, which means that finding the courage to acknowledge your shortcomings may be the first step in facing your fears. Don't let fear stop you from identifying and accepting your less than perfect qualities. Ask yourself the following question: "Am I genuinely bad at this particular thing, or am I just scared of doing it?"

Many of us think we're genuinely bad at something when we aren't. In many cases, we're only bad at it because we're running away from it or failed to properly face it in the past. Are your shortcomings disguises for fears you're trying to avoid, or are they legitimate flaws you can accept and move on from? The answer is within, and you'll find out if you're fully honest with yourself. In any case, allow your weaknesses to guide you.

For many of us, pride stops us from fully acknowledging our flaws. We're afraid of being perceived as weak, or we're scared of showing our vulnerability to others. This causes us to become defensive whenever someone points out our shortcomings or threatens our self-image. Have you noticed that defensiveness is usually a sign of denial? (Thank you, chapter 6.) When someone points out a weakness you haven't yet accepted, this hurts your feelings. By learning to embrace your flaws, however, you'll reduce your ego and diminish your fears. You'll be happier with yourself, which will allow you to drop the defensiveness and accept constructive criticism without feeling hurt. It's legit like throwing glitter on the hunchback of *all* your problems (glitter not included).

Have you ever felt inadequate because of a weakness? If so, you may feel ashamed and try to hide it. You may even feel that people would no longer accept you if they discovered your little secret. Well, it's more likely than not that there are millions of people who have the same secret. When you embrace your weaknesses, you can welcome the help and input of others without getting defensive. You can consider their opinions and be willing to change or accept criticism without feeling the need to react. You simply own your weaknesses and see others as part of your growth rather than potential threats.

Embracing your weaknesses allows you to build stronger connections with others. People will appreciate the fact that you're willing to show your vulnerability. They'll also value your authenticity and admire the fact that you have the courage to be yourself. Embracing your weaknesses and sharing your true self will make others feel comfortable doing the same with you. You'll start to see the people around you opening up and sharing their weaknesses and struggles with you. This will allow you to build stronger, deeper, and more meaningful connections with them and more effectively solve problems as they arise.

So, what are you waiting for? Start embracing your weaknesses today! Whether you choose to work on your problem areas or accept them, don't be afraid to share more of yourself with the world. We must embrace pain and our weaknesses and burn them as fuel for our journey.

Healing Vortex within Exercise

Start by making a list of your strengths and weaknesses. It's simple. Just start by listing your strengths and weaknesses. Is one list longer than the other? Why? Are you being honest and letting yourself own it all, strengths and weaknesses alike? Do you need practice seeing your strengths? Or your weaknesses? Approach this list like you're an investigator—just trying to gather all the facts and lay them out for a good look.

Start small. Just one at a time. Use one of your strengths more in your daily life—in your career, parenting, relationships with others, and hobbies. Then set a goal for how you will improve a weakness. Give yourself time, and you will grow. You can even ask yourself, is this weakness actually a strength? For example, I initially thought my bleeding heart and empathic, sensitive soul were a weakness. In fact, I was often told that I was "too sensitive" or "too emotional" or shamed for having deep empathy for others. Now I know that's a strength. Not only that, but now I *choose* to see it as a strength time and time again; and doing so frees me of past hurts. Not all weaknesses work this way, but I bet at least one or two of your weaknesses are strengths if you take a second look at them. It's called the reframe in therapy. Choose to reframe at least one of your weaknesses *now*.

Our strengths and weaknesses change with life's circumstances and as we choose to grow. We can choose to strengthen our strengths and improve our weaknesses. And sometimes life helps us do this too. We're given circumstances that make us grow in new ways, develop new strengths, and overcome old weaknesses.

But it's a choice each of us must make every day. Choose to grow, my friends. Choose to see what *it is*! Choose to embrace your strengths and your weaknesses, to say with comfort and confidence, "These are my strengths," and "These are my areas of improvement." Choose not to judge yourself but rather to openly see and accept where you are. Then choose to grow a little bit more every day. Practice saying these healing-vortex-within mantras to embrace weaknesses or rather areas of improvement and transmute them into empowerment now:

"I am aware of the areas of improvement in my life, and I take action to find solutions of the highest good."

"Weaknesses are really just areas of improvement!"

"Accepting my problems is an act of self-love and a powerful portal to solve them."

CHAPTER 9

The Portals of the Ego, Soul, and Spirit

Starve an ego; feed a soul.
—Unknown

Who is driving the bus in your life? Is it your spirit, soul, or ego? You see, our damn egos can cause a lot of trouble if we let them. No one knows this better than this troublemaking starseed indigo rebel earth angel. I like to question authority, and I spent a great deal of my life making things harder for myself because I used to let my ego make all the decisions. Once I could leave my ego at the door life truly became much easier, and I felt far more empowered to heal and deal with any challenges life threw my way. Inner-standing there is a difference between our egos, souls, and spirits will also help you.

The Ego (the Human Self, Mind, or Psyche)

Ego can mean a lot of different things. Regarding self-healing, we can inner-stand ego as how we view ourselves. It can also be called our self-image or self-concept, which is a complex set of ideas about what kind of people we are. If we have a positive self-concept, we think of ourselves as good and worthwhile people. If we have a negative self-concept, we think of ourselves as inferior or unworthy. Often ego damage and lasting ego wounds can happen in childhood or traumatic situations.

When I say to leave your ego at the door, I mean to be cognizant that healing can happen on any level, and the outcome may not be as your ego expects it to be. In fact, our egos often get in the way of letting go, positive change, and the healing process. The ego is the human part of us that sees itself as separate, as us versus them. It's like sunbeams thinking they are separate from the sun or waves thinking they are separate from the ocean. We are each a wave from the same ocean and a sunbeam from the same sun.

The ego is often driven by a core fear, which dictates how we see the world. When we live in our egos, we are controlled by our fears. When we live in a world of fear, we are living in the shadow and neglecting the light, positive aspects of ourselves and life itself. The ego isn't all bad though. We need our egos for survival. The ego is the part of us that keeps us from crossing the street when a bus is coming or helps us to remember to pay our bills on time. It serves an important function for practical human matters.

Life flows more easily when our egos support the wisdom in our souls and spirits. We must be willing to fully release and let go of our unhealed self-image and give up personal or ego gains regarding our healing. Healing first occurs energetically, and if we are too caught up in our egos' wants and needs, we may miss the subtle shifts in our vibrations.

The Soul (Our Ancient, Wise, Eternal Self)

The soul is the part of us that never dies. It is carried from lifetime to lifetime. It is our ancient, wise, eternal self—a combination of all the self-healing superpowers and all the soul gifts we have mastered over all our past lives. While it has wisdom, the soul can also carry trauma, karmic patterns from past experiences, and painful imprints that linger into the next body or energy system. The dark night of the soul is one such example of this, and it is a pivotal part of the healing journey. Feelings of extreme loss or crumbling allow the ego to loosen its grip, which leaves space for the spirit to intervene.

The Spirit (Our Divine Self, The Higher Self)

The spirit is our divine connection to the universe, to light energy and the cosmos. The spirit is our higher self. It is a higher octave of the soul.

When our hearts burst open to healing, a magical space is created for the soul to come through. When the soul bursts open, it allows the spirit to come through. When spirits, souls, and egos are able to work in harmony, we can truly tap into our unique self-healing superpowers. Getting to know and differentiate between the voices of our egos, souls, and spirits is extremely helpful when it comes to the healing vortex journey.

Get activated in your healing process by checking your ego and accepting and aligning with your soul and higher self (spirit) with these healing-vortex-within mantras:

> "I choose to let my soul and spirit guide me."
> "My higher self has all the answers I need."
> "I hear the voice of my ego, but I act on the voice of my soul—my intuition."

CHAPTER 10

The Portal of Surrender

Try something different. Surrender.
—Rumi

Probably the most common block to healing is a psychological reversal, which is the subconscious condition of self-sabotage. It literally means one's energy runs backward or scrambles when one thinks about healing. It is understandable when you think about all the things healing represents—changing, confronting fears or insecurities, examining addictive or harmful behaviors, grieving, addressing past traumas, and going through all the anxiety and fear of releasing the old to allow this new version of you to emerge. A client will say in all sincerity that they want to heal, but the energy I can sense emanating from the person's body contradicts their stated intention. That doesn't mean the person is lying; it means there is an inner conflict that needs to be settled before their mind, body, spirit, and subtle energy system will align itself with healing.

Self-sabotage and fear of success or fear of change are often the largest roadblocks to healing and awakening. Think about the energy of self-sabotage and fear; it inhibits us from action and consistency. How many of us have gone on a diet only to find ourselves with our hands in the cookie jar a few days later.

You can sabotage your health, success, and longevity by pushing too hard. Surrender is the antidote to stress in a world that relentlessly conspires to interrupt progress and wellness. Surrender boosts your brain's endorphins—euphoric, opiate-like painkillers—and serotonin, a natural antidepressant that allows you to relax, have more fun, and succeed more wildly than ever before. Though surrender may seem counterintuitive to making your goals happen, it can be the magical factor that facilitates this and relieves gridlock. Life becomes easier and more blissful when you can let go.

Surrender isn't quitting. To quit means to stop and not go back. Surrender isn't giving up. To give up means to stop trying. To give in means to yield. It is flexible, and flexibility is strength. We raise our hands in surrender, a gesture of supplication, as we humbly ask for help. There is an element of elevation in it; we must lift up to hand over. In surrendering we don't change our intention or principles. We don't change who we are or what we believe in. We realize only that we have reached our limits in the moment. We have done all we can for now. Surrender is an attitude of being and doing our best, then giving the rest to our higher power, whatever we conceive that to be.

Sometimes it seems we are forced—by circumstances, other people, demands of life, and our own bodies—to stop and rest and/or rethink our options or course of action. But all these factors are part of being human. It's not a sign of weakness but one of strength and intelligence to know when to keep going and when to take a break. We need renewal to keep going longer and function more efficiently over time.

Surrender is a choice. And true power is always a choice. In surrender we come to a moment of judgment, where we must decide whether it's more destructive or more constructive to continue what we are doing. We must weigh potential gain against possible loss and decide what best serves our purpose. The honor in surrender is in giving ourselves over to what we most value in the moment, in making a conscious, deliberate choice to be true to ourselves in the best and worst of circumstances, regardless of results. Use these healing-vortex-within mantras to engage in the magic and power of surrender:

> "I am willing to surrender."
> "I surrender and trust the process of healing and awakening."
> "I surrender all that is out of my control."

Supercharged Soul-Full Self-Care Portals

Self-care is how you take your power back.
—Lalah Delia

You've probably heard that expression *self-care* used before. I kind of, totally, hate the term—and clients often hate it too. Sometimes it's so hard to take care of ourselves, and when the term *self-care* comes up so often, it begins to become a cliché to the point that people balk at it. Many people have heard the term but don't know what it means. "Self-care, like brushing my teeth? Is that what you mean?" clients often say.

What the hell is this self-care you speak of? How do you supercharge your self-care when you struggle to do basic self-care tasks? Self-care is any activity we do deliberately to take care of our mental, emotional, physical, and spiritual health. Although it's a simple concept in theory, it's something we very often overlook. Self-care is something that recharges us rather than depletes us. Self-care isn't selfish either. Remember: you must put your oxygen mask on before you can help someone else in the event of a plane crash—or else you're both dead. Self-care is something you actively plan rather than something that just happens. It's an active choice, and you must treat it as such.

Most of us have heard about self-care. We know it's important. We may even know a few things we should do for self-care. But one of the things I especially hear over and over from clients is, "How do I fit self-care into my already-packed day?" This is such a valid question.

You're not alone if you're asking yourself this same question. Many of us tend to prioritize our day-to-day duties in something like the following order: family, work, chores (cooking, shopping, laundry, and so forth), activities or other commitments, and finally self-care. Rinse and repeat. We consistently set self-care as our lowest priority. When it's last on the list, it's the one that can most easily be skipped entirely if we run out of time.

So what happens when we don't fit self-care into our daily schedule? I don't know about you, but I know when I'm not making time or prioritizing self-care into my day, my patience level heads south. It's much easier to become snippy and less understanding when interacting with others. What else happens when self-care isn't part of our daily lives? What are the consequences of not practicing self-care? The list can include the following:

- Low energy
- Feelings of hopelessness
- Less patience
- Increased headaches
- Stomachaches and other physical symptoms of stress
- Difficulties in falling and staying asleep
- Challenges in choosing healthy food and urges to eat "comfort" foods
- Worsening mental health symptoms like depression or anxiety
- Feeling burnout
- Difficulty concentrating
- Strain or distance in the relationship with your spouse or partner
- Less patience with your children or pets
- Reduced performance at work
- Less motivation to engage in social activities
- Too many more to even list

It's no surprise that when we neglect our own self-care, it catches up with us. All the above symptoms and consequences that happen when we don't take time to better care for ourselves can add up quickly. Have you noticed any of these consequences or a lack of self-care in yourself? Maybe you have but aren't sure how to change it. Changing habits we've been stuck in for a long time can be challenging. But we *can* do it. We will do it. We are choosing to do it *now*.

The best way to make any behavioral change is to make it as simple as possible, realistic, and achievable—*and* make it come from the soul. What does this mean? It means making sure you're not expecting something that isn't going to be feasible in your day-to-day life and making sure your self-care activities are *soul-care*. For instance, brushing my teeth every day doesn't do much for my soul. I do it so I can keep that pearly white smile and eat food. Soul-*full* self-care activities will often look different, feel different, and have much more significant results when we engage in them regularly. For example, my soul-*full* self-care activities include, but are not limited to, playing with my cats, chilling in my rose garden, quoting RuPaul, exploring caves in nature, writing a standup comedy routine I will never perform (most likely), star bathing, having disco dance parties, and doing comedic karaoke.

Below is a list of soul-*full* self-care ideas. Choose even one item you think you could squeeze into your day. Maybe try to implement something in the morning so you know you won't run out of time before you have a chance to do it. The key here is just to try. Are you going to do it perfectly every day? Of course not. Maybe you try one of these ideas, and it just doesn't give you the soul-full boost you are hoping for. Then try another idea below. Keep trying until you find something that gives you the result you're looking for.

Pay attention to how you feel after you take time to attend to yourself. What do you notice in the rest of your day? Are you finding you are calmer and more patient with others? Are you sleeping better at night? The more we do something, the more likely it is to become a positive habit. This is the secret of self-care: making it a habit so it's something we wouldn't second-guess doing, just like eating dinner is something we don't typically feel guilty prioritizing.

Soul-*Full* Self-Care Ideas

- Make a deeper-meaning gratitude list from the soul for the soul
- Listen to upbeat or relaxing music that lets you tap into your intuitive center
- Take five minutes to sit down and check in with your soul
- Hug a tree or get out in nature for ten to fifteen minutes (or more)

- Give your body and soul an Epsom salt bath
- Schedule a date night with your soul mate, spouse, partner, or friends
- Enjoy a hot cup of tea you know makes your soul happy
- Spend five minutes taking deep breaths and connecting to your eternal essence within.
- Turn your phone off for thirty minutes and just be present with yourself
- Write in a journal for five minutes what your soul wants you to know (don't think too much; just let your soul answer on the page)
- Read a book for twenty minutes or an article online that lights you up or inspires you
- Unfollow someone on social media who is negative or makes you feel bad to better protect your energy and soul.
- And if you still find soul-*full* self-care difficult, silly, or hard to even begin, say these healing-vortex-within mantras to honor your soul-*full* self-care journey now:

"Self-care isn't selfish; it's a necessity for survival."
"Self-care makes me feel better, and I choose to feel better now."
"There is always time to take care of my soul."

CHAPTER 12

The Portal of Paradox

Sometimes we have to get lost before we can find ourselves.
—Vironika Tugaleva

Life is full of paradoxes, which are seemingly absurd or contradictory truths. The world is full of so many quirky and ironic paradoxes that it can make you laugh and discover profound lessons along the way. Sometimes we feel lost on our healing and awakening portal adventures before we find the soul-aligned path. We need to slow down to speed up in life; stepping away or taking a break when you are super busy helps increase productivity. When you finish your to-do list and then finish doing nothing, what should be done now?

I find it quite beautiful in a weird way that the healing and awakening journey is never truly done no matter how much hard work you do. There's always more to refine, learn, and explore along the healing vortex journey and the many portals we journey through on the regular. I used to find this fact frustrating. If the work can never be done, then what's the point of doing it at all? Now I realize there's no point, and that's the point—another paradox here but let a hoe for paradoxical healing explain. By saying, "There is no point, and that's the point," I am referring to a point as in a destination, and I'm referring to not having a destination (*point* on a map); there is always a journey that gives limitless space and time for expansion. If there were the illusion of an endpoint, we would surrender our search for deeper levels of healing and awakening and existential awareness. This open-ended journey within catalyzes the inspiration for continued growth and progress in expanding your inner and outer worlds.

When we ascend to higher levels of personal and spiritual development within, it's not a linear progression like finishing chapters in a book and never reading them again. Oh no! The events and people in our lives, those that come to teach us, happen in cycles corresponding to celestial energy cycles like the new or full moon every month. What we already learned can swing back around and return to our lives in a different form. Similar to reading a book, just because you've finished it once doesn't mean you have absorbed the entire truth it possesses. Trust me on this one. I have reread many of the same books again at different stages of my life, and I am always inspired when I can extrapolate deeper wisdom from the same text. Be willing to embrace and accept these paradoxes along your healing vortex journey and know you will continue to reach new heights and deeper portals along the way.

Another paradox of healing and awakening worth diving into now is that both can be hard and painful work that is easy to avoid or something you want to rush through—the old paradigm—and at the same time, healing and awakening can also be fun. Healing is fun? I know some people reading this are immediately going to roll their eyes at the statement that healing can be fun, but hear me out on this one. Who the f said healing and awakening have to be this gross, miserable, boring, painful experience? That is a false belief implanted in our brains by antiquated systems that treat the symptoms not the root and keep people dependent on their pain and fear so they will spend money on quick fixes and useless material junk. Yes, there is pain involved in becoming more conscious and aware, but suffering is optional. People will do anything, no matter how absurd to avoid facing their soul—because most people believe healing is *always* hard and *only* painful. I am here to tell you in more portal chapters than one, honey, that this inner journey is what you make of it.

Healing is fun when you allow it to be. Think about the last time you had a deep belly laugh or the last time you played with a pet or child or with your friends. Those things are healing and fun and simple. I love to laugh and make healing sessions with my clients fun. When a client and I get to laughing, I can tell they are in the healing vortex fully, and they inner-stand that *life is too serious to be taken seriously all the time*! This truth also applies to healing and awakening and, most importantly, the ongoing journey that is life. We need to laugh, play, and not just focus on the hard parts; this makes the process much more enjoyable and sustainable since it is a lifelong journey and beyond as well.

We need to live life and not always focus on the healing part. We also need to make time to heal and find activities that light up our souls. Sometimes not focusing so much on healing and awakening or forcing it to happen make it happen. The paradox of healing and awakening is just one of many in life. We must accept and embrace these paradoxes and learn how to utilize them for our greater good. This makes the whole process less painful and more sustainable. Remember: healing and awakening are lifelong endeavors—so let's make them enjoyable, at least some of the time.

There is a common misconception that healing is a one-time deal. As you will see, healing can be quick and easy, but it is also a beautiful part of the human experience throughout our entire lives. Healing and wellness for the mind, body, and spirit are some of the most enchantingly magical and lifelong processes we are gifted with in this plane of existence. Once you allow yourself to deeply inner-stand this and accept healing as a normal, ongoing part of your life (just like eating, shitting, and paying taxes), you will dissolve all false beliefs around healing being finite. While healing is a normal and ongoing part of life, it can also be quick and easy. Notice when negative thinking creeps in and simply forgiving the thought and choosing a new, better thought. For example, you notice yourself complaining and think, *Why is life so hard?* Or, *I can never do anything right.* Become aware of how unhelpful those types of thoughts are and choose again. You can choose a new, neutral, or positive thought instantaneously like, *I'm going to get through this* or *even though life is hard right now, I have people who love me to help ease the stress.* Healing toxic thoughts, unwanted feelings, or destructive behaviors can be that easy.

Smile, laugh, and play every day and say these healing vortex mantras daily. Say them in a funny voice (if that helps you have more fun with it). Turn away from any distractions for a moment, relax your jaw, roll back and lower your shoulders, relax your stomach, and say these healing-vortex-within mantras as often as needed:

> "Healing and awakening are paradoxical in nature, and I am cool with that."
> "I accept healing into my life today and every day."
> "I inner-stand that healing is a normal, ongoing and beautiful part of life."

CHAPTER 13

Your INNER-G Portal

Everything is energy, and that's all there is to it. Match the
frequencies of the reality you want, and you cannot help but get
that reality. It can be no other way. This isn't philosophy.
This is physics.
—Albert Einstein

You create everything you experience. In other words, you create your
own reality. Your external world isn't separate from you, but it is directly
connected to you. There is an energetic and spiritual force that connects
everything in this universe. And it is through this connected energy of all
things seen and unseen that you create your reality. This powerful creative
energy that emanates from inside you molds and shapes the universe
around you.

Quantum physics teaches us that energy cannot be created or
destroyed—it simply changes form. Energy is in constant fluctuations
within you right now and externally in your environment. Your thoughts
and feelings are waves of energy. The sensations in your body are waves
of energy. You probably just blinked right now. Then you smiled and
thought, *Dr. Heather is funny…weird but funny.* Now you're probably
thinking, *Is this bitch reading my mind or what?* Neural signals are firing
left and right in your brain—*peeewww, peeewww, peeeeeewwwwww, ping.*
That's the sound neurons make. Trust me, I'm a doctor. Another blink,
another smile. See, more energy is in constant motion and flux, baby.

Let's look more closely at how you are using your energy. Ask yourself
whether you feel blocked, stagnant, or not aligned with the energy you'd
like to be experiencing. Say to yourself, "What does my energy feel like

right now? How would I describe my physical, mental, emotional, and spiritual energies in this exact moment? Is my energy going in the direction I would like it to?" Take a few minutes to answer these questions honestly and specifically.

Energy goes where your attention flows. Energy follows your focus. Do you have a direction or intention you focus on regarding your energy? Or do you just allow energy to permeate into you from everywhere? As a third dimensional expression of energy in a meat skeleton, you interact with energy all day long through your thoughts, words, emotions, and environment. Thoughts, words, emotions, and all environments are energy. Every thought and emotion you have sends out energy waves. Even if your external environment or internal landscape isn't what you desire it to be, how your energy vibrates now impacts both your internal and external experiences.

Let's dive a little deeper into this cosmic energy discussion now. You may want to read this more than once. When your energy vibrates (in other words, you consciously decide to be in a specific energetic state) in peace, love, and harmony, you create alignment and flow of energy to what it is you are giving attention. When you vibrate in anger, conflict, and disharmony, you create pain and the feeling of separation to what it is you are giving attention to. Remember: how you focus your energy impacts what you create internally and externally.

I will never forget one morning in 2015 when I was running late to work at a well-known, fancy-schmancy "institution" in San Francisco that shall remain unnamed so my ass doesn't get sued. I made an illegal left-hand turn at the same intersection where I had made an illegal left-hand turn every morning for nearly two years, commuting way across town from where I lived to get to a job I hated. *Weeooo weeeooo* go the red and blue lights, and next thing you know, I'm holding a traffic ticket in hand and even later to this toxic work environment than I had been initially. I made a conscious decision at that moment not to let this *very* expensive ticket and dumpster fire of a job ruin my entire day. *Yeah*, I thought, *I'm going to practice what I preach and choose the thoughts and energy that are in the highest vibrational state of love and service I can generate right now.*

I started saying my mantras and reminding myself of all the things I was so grateful for and all the clients I loved working with, even if the people in positions of power were terrible. I was lucky to be alive and housed and employed and living in a gorgeous city. I was so grateful to have a vehicle to get to work so I could sleep in late. I started to thank every little thing I saw during my drive to work—from the rain on my windshield to the homeless guy taking a dump on the street to the Mac Dre songs I was playing loud while rapping along and enjoying my last minutes of alone time before going back into the trenches of community mental health.

Once I got to work, to my surprise I found a parking spot right in front like a miracle from the parking gods. My energy was already working for me rather than against me because I had acted to raise my vibe back into alignment with love and service. I wasn't even *that* late; maybe no one would notice me slip in, and today would be a good day after all. And then something *really* special happened. When I got out of my car and looked up at the sky, the sprinkle rain mist stopped, and the sun peeked out just enough that a glorious full rainbow emerged over the building across the street. It was one of the most powerful signs I have ever received from Iris, the Goddess of Rainbows, and she be sending me a whole hell of a lot of magical rainbow signs, dude. "Fully, yas gawd!" I remember saying that aloud on the street with a big smile. This was extra special, and I always remember that day when I'm out of alignment with the energy of love and service and fun and magic. And rainbows, honey! Your energy creates your reality—literally.

Your thoughts and especially your emotions determine what kind of waves of energy you are sending out into the universe. What you send out through your vibration always comes back as your reality. The mirror of cosmic energy truly is your friend, since it is letting you know and showing you how you are using your energy. Direct your attention and intention in a way that is harmonious mentally, emotionally, and spiritually with what you desire. Recognize your thoughts, what you pay attention to, and how your experience impacts your environment.

Just as you don't need to inner-stand the law of gravity before you can fall, you don't need to completely grasp the concept of energy (INNER-G) healing before you dive into the practice. If you truly inner-stood just how powerful your energy is, you would be able to manifest anything, heal anything, and awaken anything within just by changing your energetic vibe. How do you think people find love or get the record deal or finally find the courage to leave a bad relationship or stop smoking or start exercising or forgive someone who harmed them? They change their thoughts, feelings, and behaviors, all of which are *energy*. And you can too. Start practicing with mantras and gratitude, then kick it up a notch and write down some manifestations or make a vision board. Go after your goals and dreams with love and high vibe energy. You got this.

Practice Creating Your Reality

Real badass mofos create their reality; they tap into their INNER-G on a regular basis. Before you start your day, find a few minutes to sit quietly with your eyes closed. Relax your body and begin to become aware of your thoughts, clearing your mind space of unconscious thinking. Breathe and connect with your INNER-G. Visualize a unicorn riding a motorcycle if that helps (that's what my INNER-G looks like, but yours can look like anything or anyone you so desire). When you are completely relaxed and alert, use the following process to bring your desire into your reality.

Practice using these healing-vortex-within mantras anytime you need to shift your energy or remind yourself how incredibly powerful your energy is in creating your reality:

> "MY INNER-G creates my reality."
> "I choose to align my INNER-G with the highest vibrational state and unlock my inner badass."
> "I focus my INNER-G on what I want to feel and create in my life."

CHAPTER 14

The Portal of Intuition

Intuition is seeing with the soul.
—Deane Koontz

So what exactly *is* intuition? I often refer to intuition as the "voice of the soul." Our intuition is a loving inner voice that always guides us toward positive actions and soul-aligned outcomes. You've experienced it before, even if you didn't notice. It's that gut feeling that steers us in the right direction, even when we're not always aware of it. Intuition can sometimes sound like a whisper in our ear or like a thought that lands just a little bit different than other thoughts.

Our intuition is the way our higher selves or our souls speak to us. It's our souls guiding us. When we learn to listen and trust our intuition, it's like unlocking a cool superpower that can help us lead a more fulfilling life. Even though intuition is cosmically stellar and always serves our highest good, it can feel *so* hard to trust it, especially at first.

Your intuition can also be thought of as your "inner tuition" or the internal charge for teaching or instruction. Tuition is a sum of money charged for teaching or instruction by a school, college, or university. Luckily, your intuition isn't mailing you a bill or anything. Our intuition does have an "internal charge," which our bodies or minds receive in the form of inner guidance or inner knowing. This is how the voice of our souls instructs and teaches us what we need to know to skillfully navigate our lives. It's like the GPS system of our souls.

In today's world where logic is king, knowing how to trust your intuition can be tricky.

Even if you want to use your intuition more, the daily hustle and bustle of life can make it hard to feel any sort of spiritual guidance. Learning how to travel down the portal of intuition and learning to trust your intuition can help with the little things in life and the big stuff—like how to live a more super-awesome life filled with so much joy that you want to dance in the streets. Intuition is our natural state. Believe it or not, intuition isn't some weird or woo-woo thing. Being intuitive is our natural state. We all have intuition—you, me, the gal who pours our coffee at the diner, and even our pet cat. The problem is, we don't always listen. But it's not our fault—we've been conditioned by society to trust logic and not to put too much emphasis on what we feel or sense. If you haven't trusted your intuition for a long time, don't worry. It hasn't gone away. It's always there within you. It is your essence—your soul—and it can't be separated from you. It's always there, and it's never too late to trust it and start listening. It just takes a little practice to learn how.

Ways to Trust Your Intuition

When you start traveling down the portal of intuition and following the tips below, you'll start to feel a little less detached from your intuitive guidance. And slowly but surely, you'll start becoming more aware of the voice of your soul—your intuition. Remember that learning how to trust your intuition takes practice. Have patience with yourself and have fun.

Slow Down—Stop. Yes, stop. Make space for quiet time and reflection. I know it's hard. You need to make dinner. Or work or study. The kids spilled their lasagna on your new rug. I know, but this is important. This is your joy we're talking about here. This is about you feeling connected to and supported by your soul. The first step toward learning how to trust your intuition is to let your brain rest and focus inward. What do you feel? Why? Work on being present with your soul's voice of intuition. How does it feel in your soul? We are so programmed to always be doing. But doing or spinning in circles isn't the same as taking inspired action. If you feel you are spinning in circles, it's a good clue that you are trying to do it all on your own and not letting your intuition guide you. Think less. Feel more. Tricky, I know. But as you stop doing and start being more, it gets easier. Take note of what feels right and true for you instead of what you believe to be reasonable or what you have been told is right.

Get Out in Nature—Spend time in nature, taking in the beauty of the earth. Take time to appreciate the quiet and peace. Trusting our intuition is *much* easier when we allow our minds to quiet. Nature can help us more easily connect with our hearts and instincts. Sit outside or go for a walk in the park. Go wild—hug a tree! When we connect to ourselves in the here and now, our intuition will speak to us, and we will be able to hear it.

Meditate—Meditate by simply focusing on your breath, bringing your mind back to your breath whenever you notice your mind has started thinking again. And it *will* ... that's what our minds do. There are hundreds, if not thousands, of ways to meditate. *Find one that works for you.* Try a guided meditation, a standing or sitting meditation, or a visualization if you are more of a visual person. Meditation *is* for everyone, so keep trying until you find the style that suits you best (more on this in the meditation portal chapter). With practice and patience, you will begin to quiet the mind more often so you can hear your higher self and that voice of your soul—your intuition.

Get Creative—One of the most fun ways to learn how to trust your intuition is to be creative. Even if you don't think you're creative, I bet you can be. When you are being creative, you encourage the non-logical aspect of your soul to be open to the things your rational mind can't even fathom. You don't need to be Picasso (or Pricasso) to be creative. You can write, do scrapbooking, paint, design curtains, do woodworking—whatever you enjoy. Personally, my creativity comes in the form of coloring, decorating my home, and finding new ways to be weird in my backyard. You can do anything in a creative way; try it the next time you do something mundane, like paying bills or cleaning. Add a creative flair and check in with your intuition along the way.

Know That Inspiration *Is* Intuition—Have you ever felt *so* inspired or passionate about something? Like you just *have* to dress up in a unicorn onesie and stand on your block, yelling "Pickles!"? Everyone gets inspired in different ways, but that is just one example I will elaborate on in a future chapter of how I portal to my soul's voice. It may have been some time, but you have been inspired before, and getting inspired again now will help you tap into your intuition. Inspiration is one way your intuition speaks to you. In fact, the word *inspiration* literally translates to "in spirit"; when you are inspired, you are in your spirit and you can more effectively hear the voice of your soul, your intuition. One of the easiest ways to learn how to trust your intuition is to follow your inspired feelings. Does the idea light you up when you think about starting a blog? Do it! Does the thought of volunteering at the local food pantry make your heart sing? Whatcha waitin' for? Remember: our intuition wants to guide us to our highest good—that place where we will be happy and peacefully open to the wonders of life.

Raise Your Vibration—We are all energetic, spiritual beings who vibrate at certain frequencies. When your vibration is high, you feel happy. Saying "raise your vibration" is like a fancy way of saying to do what makes you happy. Raising your vibration makes it easier to tune into what your intuition is telling you and allows inspired ideas and solutions to come to you.

Start Small—When you are first learning how to trust your intuition, it can seem like you'll never figure it out. Is this my intuition? Is this my mind? Ugh! Forget it. I'm just going to ask someone what I should do. Start small. Ask your intuition for some guidance. That's a small step. Once you begin trusting and noticing how good it feels, your confidence in your intuition will build, and you'll use it every day in every decision you make. Your intuition is a powerful portal on the healing and awakening journey of life, and as you learn to connect to your intuition on a deeper level, you will see the tremendous benefit it can bring to you and others.

Use these healing-vortex-within mantras to further support accessing your portal of intuition:

> "I choose to listen to my intuition every day and take inspired action when needed."
> "I am turning the volume up on my intuition now."
> "I trust the inner charge of my intuition so I don't pay the cost of ignoring it."

CHAPTER 15

The Portal of Intentions: Activating the Healing Vortex Within

> Each intention sets energy into motion. What you intend is what
> you become. Power is energy that is formed by the intentions of
> the soul. It is light shaped by the intentions of love and compassion
> guided by wisdom. It is energy that is focused and directed
> toward the fulfilment of the tasks of the soul upon the Earth.
> —Gary Zukav

When it comes to doing any sort of healing, energetic, or spiritual work, it is most effective by starting with setting crystal-clear intentions. Intention is a way to redirect your energy into where you want it to go rather than into where you are now. This doesn't mean you should think only positive thoughts. It simply means you need to know what you truly intend for yourself. It's like committing to a goal. The portal of intentions sends a message to your mind, body, and spirit to activate the healing vortex within, which essentially means you are flipping on the light switch of your soul.

If you find it hard to imagine how powerful intent is, remember that your brain is a very powerful processing machine. We still have lots to discover about it, but you can think up to seventy thousand thoughts a day and process huge amounts of sensory information. This means that a lot of what you think—which directly impacts how you feel—is automatic and that your mind filters information at a dizzying rate. When you set a clear, positive intention, you help your mind to realign with that intention. An intention is a thought initially and your thoughts create your reality.

Intention setting is incredibly powerful and essentially provides your energetic body and subconscious mind with a road map, pointing to where you want to be. Setting intentions also helps your energetic and spiritual body—your higher self or true self—to emerge. This is the part of you that is truly made up of love and has only the best intention for you. When you are in a painful situation, connecting to this part of yourself can be hard.

So, how do you set an intention? Create your intention with positive energy and love.

Intentions, which are based on your recovery, growth, and healing, will be the most effective and give you the best long-term results. Our intentions are *every-thang*! Not a single thing in your life or on this planet can be accomplished without intention; that is how powerful intentions are. You can create your own intention by writing down what you feel your core needs are, or you can use this intention as a starting point. "My intention is to heal from my childhood trauma and move into a new phase of thriving in my life." Or this one is great too: "My intention is to be a badass mofo."

It can be helpful to write the above intention (or your version of it, one that's personal to you) in a journal as well as in other places where you will regularly see it. This could be setting intentions for the week or a long-term goal. You can put some notes around the house or keep one in your bag or somewhere you will see it at work so you can be reminded of your intention throughout the day.

To invoke the healing vortex energy within, say this invocation aloud: "Thank you, universe and the healing powers within me, for activating now. Please surround me in light and healing energy. Help me to clear my physical, mental, emotional, and spiritual being from negativity in all its forms. Release any dense or toxic energy within my being into the light and help me to stay grounded, centered, and present in the energy of love. Help me to start making healthy choices in the present moment to restore my natural, radiant state of well-being. Help keep me aligned with my soul, my self-healing superpowers, and the voice of my intuition to set intentions and manifest outcomes for the highest good of all. Thank you. Thank you. Thank you."

Allow yourself to sit calmly in silence, or if you like, write down any insights, intentions, or realizations that were energetically received. Make sure to take some small action on the intentions you set and intuitive gifts you may have received in this exercise. When you invoke the healing power of the universe within your soul, you will receive the support you need, often in the form of seeing the steps you can take to heal yourself. Be sure to act on any intuitive nudges you receive. You may also want to simply ask your body what it needs to heal and then take action to align yourself with the positive state you seek. Be patient with yourself if you feel this exercise is challenging and remember that with practice your intuition's voice becomes clearer and louder, and your intentions will gain power and clarity. You can also use these healing-vortex-within mantras to help gain clarity and motivation for intention setting:

> "I am setting clear and realistic intentions for my healing and awakening journey."
> "I am setting intentions for the best possible outcome for all."
> "I choose to set clear and specific intentions that align with the energy of empowerment, love, and respect for myself and others."

CHAPTER 16

Galvanizing Portals of Abundance

We don't create abundance. Abundance is
always present. We create limitations.
—Arnold Patent

You hear a lot of people in the healing and spiritual communities pushing things like abundance and manifestation like they were the next best things since sliced bread. Don't get me wrong; manifestation and abundance are obviously wonderful concepts. I just think there are so many distortions and instant-gratification schemes out there that they confuse us all. If we get too confused and overwhelmed, we can easily become depleted and not be able to follow through with necessary actions to galvanize and materialize those intentions into an abundant reality. In fact, what most law of attraction junkies and manifestation buzzword addicts fail to address is that we don't create abundance—just like Arnie says in the quote. Abundance is always available to us. However, we create limitations to abundance, and this prevents the WERK required to materialize and galvanize those damn intentions.

Galvanizing means stimulating in a way that provokes action or effort. Intention without attention or action is useless. After you set your intentions, how will you focus your attention to achieve them? Intentions are like planting the seeds, but you can't just plant seeds in the spring and expect to have a boatload of pumpkin gourd homies coming harvest in the fall. You must water, fertilize, and tend to any potential issues with your garden and those planted seeds. You must feel abundant about all aspects of your garden and your life because you *are* abundant.

The same goes for the intentions you set and all intentions you will ever set on your healing and awakening journey, which is a lifelong adventure. So make damn sure you are growing the exact kind of vegetables, fruits, and flowers you want to enjoy (in other words, specific "AF" intentions). Subsequently, you best make sure you are paying attention to your newly planted garden of intentions through *action*. Attention or action on seeing those intentions through to harvest is so incredibly important, but we all make the mistake of setting goals or intentions and then not behaving, tending to, or paying attention to the action steps to ensure those intentions become a reality and real food to feast on. We might even be growing limitations instead of the abundance we seek. Use this portal of galvanizing abundance to tap into what is always available to you with clear intentions and actions. For additional support, practice using these healing-vortex-within mantras to help you galvanize portals of abundance and clear away any limitations to the abundance that is always available to us:

> "I choose to focus on practical action to galvanize my intentions."
> "I transmute all blocks to abundance, and I activate abundance in all areas of my life."
> "I am a galvanizing portal of manifestation for all I could ever want or need."

CHAPTER 17

The Portal of Protection

Protect your spirit, because you are in the place where spirits get eaten.
—John Trudell

If you are an aware person who has portaled this far in the book, you probably have heard statements in the world at large like, "We are in the middle of a spiritual or psychological war." There is no denying that we are living on a planet riddled with chaos, dense energies, and intense polarization. It is psychological warfare intended to divide us through various mind control tactics, deception, and spiritual or energetic depletion.

You've probably heard the story about the red and black ants. It goes like this: if you collect one hundred black ants and one hundred red ants and put them in a jar, nothing will happen. But if you take the jar, shake it violently, and leave it on the table, the ants will start killing each other. The red ants believe the black ants are the enemy, while the black ants believe the red ants are the enemy when the real enemy is the person who shook the jar. The same is true in society. Men versus women, left versus right, rich versus poor, faith versus science.

Before we fight each other, we must ask ourselves, "Who shook the jar?"

If you see the division as good versus bad, black versus white, or awake versus asleep, you create an internal war in your mind. The greatest illusion in this universe is that of separation. We are all connected and come from the same elements that make up the stars that were created from the Source of it *all*. If we want to save the world or save others, we end up creating a world and relationships that need saving. We must decide instead to create multiple portals to empowerment and protection where people can save, heal, and awaken themselves. We can protect our energy by practicing a healthy nonattachment to the chaos around us and by not taking on energies that don't belong to us.

The things we do and the people and the environments we are around either give us energy or drain our energy, and sometimes they can even suck the life out of our spirit. Just think about how you feel after watching the news for five minutes. For this reason, we must choose wisely and protect our energy accordingly. Traveling through these power portals of healing and awakening does take energy, and having empowering tools for protecting and clearing your energy is essential in this work and will further enhance your health in all areas of your life.

It's important to learn (and apply) tools for daily clearing of our energy field and maintaining spiritual and psychological protection. We need to take our power back instead of over-identifying with another or the dumpster fire train wrecks that don't belong to us. It's important to get centered and notice how we feel now. Overall, stepping back into our power and learning to control and protect our energy require determination and practice. It doesn't help anyone—not us and not our loved ones—if we are unable to function because of being overwhelmed.

Here are twelve examples of easy-to-use energy protection tools:

1. Wear deflecting crystals such as jet, black tourmaline, hematite, or tiger's eye. If you wear or carry these crystals, they will project their energy outward, creating a shield of protection for you.
2. Take baths with Epsom salt, sea salt, or Himalayan salt; the baths are relaxing and cleanse your energy.
3. Learn to cover your solar plexus with your hands or arms. You may even use visualization to help you do so.
4. Sage yourself as well as your space often; you can also use incense, candles, rose water, or essential oils.
5. Learn to pick up objects or use your right hand when handling an object you aren't familiar with. The left hand receives, and the right hand sends out energy.
6. Learn how to say, "No, I don't have the time" or "I am unable to help you now."

7. Activate your spiritual protection—your guides, angels, ancestors, Source frequencies, and the non-physical helpers. Ask them to protect you energetically.

8. Be sure to cut those emotional cords often with cord-cutting meditations, visualizations, or mantras below. You can also send electric violet light through energy cords that you don't want to completely severe which will enable healing and protection energy to be transmitted.

9. Receive healing treatments such as body work, massages, or any type of holistic healing treatment. When you are feeling compromised, don't perform any energy, healing, or psychic work. You are more likely to let your guard down and take on someone else's stuff.

10. Before you leave your home, pull your aura in a little closer to the body. You most certainly don't need to go out into the world wide open.

11. Use command phrases such as "Shields up!" or "I invoke a bubble of pink and gold protection around my body" or visualize a big, velvety cloak you can use to close energetically around you.

12. Use a visualization of mirrors being placed around your aura, facing outward. This will help you deflect unwanted sensations.

Know that you are safe and protected on your soul's sacred journey. For additional support, use these healing-vortex-within mantras to fully activate the portal of protection:

> "I hereby void all contracts that were entered into against my free will; my energy cannot be used for anything without my conscious consent from this point forward through eternity."
> "I cut all cords with anything or anyone that isn't in alignment with my highest good."
> "I transmute all energy that isn't mine to hold into love; I call my energy back to me now."

CHAPTER 18

The Perpetual Portal of Learning

> We learn … 10% of what we read, 20% of what we hear,
> 30% of what we see, 50% of what we both hear and see,
> 70% of what is discussed, 80% of what we experience
> personally, and 95% of what we teach to someone else.
> —William Glasser

Realize that you are always in a perpetual portal of learning. Most people think learning happens in school or from textbooks or teachers. Yet as Billy's quote up top implies, only 10 percent of learning may come from books. We learn the most through our personal experiences, our relationships with ourselves and others and what we teach or send out into the world. Learning through personal experience can be fun, inspiring, and life changing in deeply positive ways. Learning from experience can also mean getting burned badly when you touch that hot stove. Many of us have had experiences of learning things the hard way. But learning, healing, and personal growth don't need to be so hard unless we decide to make it that way.

Learning has always been my favorite hobby and pastime. Ask anyone who knows me. I get all kinds of "soulgasms" from learning something new and interesting, and I am *always* learning something new and interesting, especially through my personal experiences. It was oddly funny and concerning for many of my family members and friends when I finally got my doctorate degree and stopped going to school. "What are you going to do now? Are you going to be okay without school?" they asked me like I was some kind of school-monster-book-fiend, devouring hits of books and information for breakfast, always looking for my next fix. I'll admit it was scary to let go of the structure of graduate school after so many years. But luckily one thing I've learned is that the more information and wisdom you attain, the more you realize how little you truly know. In fact, the vast majority of information I use to help and teach others I didn't learn in school or from a textbook; I learned the most valuable lessons from personal experiences.

The most deeply healing and awakening lessons I have learned didn't happen in a classroom. In fact, one happened while I was dressed up in *full* unicorn realness at San Francisco Gay Pride Festival. It was quite the fluffy-white, pastel club kid fantasy of a unicorn costume, and I was living my best life romping around and dancing at the Civic Center Plaza when the group of friends I was with shrieked in delight when they saw a miraculous sight. It was a group of about a dozen glittery, rainbow Hula-Hooping unicorns on stilts prancing toward us at full speed. My people! *YAS!* I was so excited to see other unicorns and giant ones at that as they charged closer to us with their Hula-Hoops and tossed one over the top of me. To my horror I realized at that moment that I couldn't Hula-Hoop; I had never learned how to Hula-Hoop, and a dark wave of embarrassment and shame washed over my previously illuminated energy. I could feel the group of stilt unicorns' disappointment as they just shook their heads and galloped off into the distance.

"OMG, Heather … you don't know how to Hula-Hoop?" my friends said in shock and sadness as a glorious unicorn party opportunity was destroyed with thousands of people watching. It wasn't the best day of my life, to say the least, but what I did at that moment (aside from turning bright red and quickly changing the topic) was that I vowed to myself to learn to Hula-Hoop if it was the last thing I ever did. I had learned through years of painful experiences far worse than this glittery unicorn parade that life is too short to stay stuck in shame or not feel good enough. I chose to see that experience as a powerful motivator to learn something new and shift my pain into passion for life and my joy of learning. And you know what? I am an excellent Hula-Hoop Queen now. *YAS*, a hula hoop "QWAYNE," ya dig? I even use a weighted Hula-Hoop most days for a fun, quick way to exercise and shift my energy between client sessions. Going through an embarrassing and shameful experience wasn't going to get me down because I alchemized that low-vibe feeling into a learning experience. That is true magic, and you can do that with anything. We are always learning, and the perpetual portal of learning from life is infinite in its nooks and crannies for discovering just how strong and resilient we are.

Take five to ten minutes now and think about a recent personal experience you had where you felt embarrassed, guilty, ashamed, sad, or disappointed in yourself. How can you learn from that difficult personal experience? What was the universe trying to teach you? How can you alchemize that painful emotion into something helpful or a higher vibe in your life? Write down your findings and take one small action step to learn from life's challenges.

Anything that annoys us is teaching us patience. Anything that angers us is teaching us compassion and leading us to what we need to work on inside. Anything you fear is teaching you faith and inner strength. Anything you can't control is teaching you how to let go and live in the present moment. Be willing to be humbled by life's teachings and travel through the perpetual portal of learning time and time again. We attract the lessons our souls need to be realigned with our highest good and our truest path. Use these healing-vortex-within mantras for additional support:

> "I choose to learn from my personal experiences in life."
> "I am the teacher and the student; I enjoy learning and teaching from within."
> "The best lessons in life come from alchemizing pain into something empowering."

CHAPTER 19

Time Portals

> If you are depressed you are living in the past. If you are anxious you
> are living in the future. If you are at peace you are living in the present.
> —Lao Tzu

The past, present, and future walked into a bar—it was *tense*. I tell this funny pun to convey the stress time can trigger for many but also to get you to laugh and be lighthearted because what is time really to an eternal soul? Time is one of my favorite topics to discuss, and I am of two minds when we talk about time portals. First, time travel to the past for facilitating energy healing, inner child work, or trauma release is beyond cathartic and empowering work I do regularly for myself and my clients. We will talk more about these methods in future chapters. I also love to plan for the future and use my gift of sight and imagination to uplift others, the microcosm of my immediate world, and the macrocosm of planet earth and beyond. Working with past and future time portals in these ways is very intentional, with crystal-clear boundaries, and it is also time limited.

Time portals of the past or future and working on being more present with life transitions and new directions, are themes that often appear for those doing deep healing. Right now, you might be feeling energetically depleted, physically stagnant, or stuck—or in between choices that could be leaving you worried you'll make the wrong decision. While everything works on the cosmic clock of divine timing, we want to try to avoid waiting too long to seize opportunities. It's important to pay close attention to where we direct our personal energy since we all know we can easily get stuck in the portal of the past or trapped in a future-tripping vortex of despair.

Being aware of these different time portals and how living in the past or future affects our emotional state allows us to be more present. Your presence is your present; truly being in the here and now is a gift we often take for granted. Very few of us are ever taught how to live in the present, and consequently, we can be led down opposing paths of past or future, traversing two worlds, of which we have no control. Now, what is time when it comes to healing and awakening? The esoteric concept of time is a subject many books have been written on (and I will be writing about it in my future book, *What Is Time?*), but for now, here is a general vibe on the past, future, and present worlds we portal through every day. Innerstanding the basics on time portals will empower you significantly on this journey.

The Past Portal

If you are like most people, you are invigorated with distant memories of love and joy. Perhaps you reflect on past romances, distant lands, old friends, or small successes. But there is a flip side to reminiscing on the past. As well as elation, you probably also feel a lot of pain, regret, disappointment, and even shame. And this is also normal. It is completely human to suffer because of reflecting on the past, and we all experience this in different shapes and forms. While some of us find relief and peace in relinquishing the past and embracing the present, others of us somehow can't seem to escape from the grips of the past portal.

For some of us, the past literally consumes our entire waking lives and controls what we decide to do, say, and how we choose to be. Perhaps most regrettably, living in the past sabotages and slowly undermines our relationships with our friends, family members, children, and partners. There could be several reasons why you live in the past, such as being raised in an environment that encouraged such a habit (for example, parents who were constantly reminiscing about the past), having a genetic predisposition to depression or other similar tendencies, living in the past as a coping (or escape) mechanism to avoid the present, and developing the habit due to low self-esteem and the unconscious belief that you don't deserve to be happy.

Regardless of why you might get stuck in the past, it keeps you from taking responsibility over your happiness, your healing and awakening power, and your life. Living in the past keeps you in patterns of self-sabotage, anger, depression, regret, resentment, reliving past trauma or pain, and loss of personal power. The truth is that life is uncertain, unstable, and unpredictable. Often this realization is what promotes the habit of past dwelling: to escape what is, to preserve a false sense of control, but life cannot be put into a tightly held box. We all experience loss, but the important thing to remember is that all bad and good things in life provide us opportunities to grow and to become deeper, wiser, and stronger. Holding on to the past creates a lack of energy to be present or move forward in life in an empowered way. Living in the portal of the past gradually destroys connections to others as well. Living in the past is essentially living in death.

The Future Portal

Future tripping or obsessing and worrying about the future is also a common part of the human experience. Most people cannot help but obsess and worry about the what-ifs in life. There are infinite what-ifs, and we all know how much precious time is wasted when we get stuck in a time portal of future tripping in this way. When things don't go as planned, some people may feel high levels of anxiety or stress. This lack of control over the future can lead to destructive behaviors to try to deal with stressful situations. Wondering about the what-ifs in life tends to occur more frequently among many people who are feeling stuck, anxious, or afraid. It can be easy to constantly worry about our future and struggle when situations don't go as planned.

Future tripping can lead to destructive behaviors for many who are trying to cope with the demands of life. Obsessing and worrying about the future may lead to engaging in destructive patterns such as alcohol or substance abuse, unhealthy distractions like excessive TV watching or internet use, and binge eating, purging, or not eating at all to try to gain control back. Eating is an action many people feel they can control. Consequently, many people engage in addictive or harmful eating behaviors to try to cope with their fear of future outcomes. For many people, not having the ability to control every detail of their future inhibits them from focusing on the present moment. They become fearful of the future and obsess over negative outcomes. It is important for all of us to learn how to act in the present moment to prevent worry and fear of the future. The future depends on what you do today, so come back to now and take action today to improve your life tomorrow.

The Present Portal

Louise Hay wrote, "The point of power is always in the present." The next step in the process of present living is finding something to be consumed with right here, right now in the present moment. This most likely involves fulfilling a long-held dream, like attempting to write a book, creating a flower garden, or even cleaning out the whole house. No matter how romantic or homely your interest is, do it. If you don't have a long-held passion or plan, think of something. Even the act of researching is a form of being consumed. Occupy yourself in the present, and you won't have time to dwell in the past. "Yesterday's the past, tomorrow's the future, but today is a gift. That's why it's called the present," Bill Keane said.

Place both hands on your heart and repeat these healing-vortex-within mantras loudly and proudly as often as needed to come back to the portal of the present:

> "My presence is my present."
> "I choose to learn from the past, prepare for the future,
> and live in the present."
> "I heal the pain of the past and release the fear of the
> future by being fully present *now*."

CHAPTER 20

The Portal Less Traveled: Shadow WERK

> One does not become enlightened by imagining figures
> of light, but by making the darkness conscious.
> —Carl Jung

Healing and awakening often feel like a crisis. They can even feel like a never-ending dumpster fire train wreck at times. Healing and awakening can also feel like the most delightful summer breeze under a sky full of sparkling stars while you listen to your favorite Prince song on repeat. But a lot of the time we are just putting out one damn dumpster fire after the next. The goal is to be the best damn dumpster fire putter outer you've ever seen. The dark night of the soul is a deep-seated human experience that can be incredibly traumatic, filled with sadness and melancholy. Trust me, I know.

This is an incredibly trying time in the human experience, one filled with ongoing emotional turmoil, grief and loss, instability, and chaos. Sometimes the most insignificant event can spiral an individual into a dark-night experience. It may seem as if the world is crashing down around you, but just as night turns into day, it is a cycle of rebirth and renewal. Like the earth's cycle of the night, it is always darkest just before the dawn. Know that you will be emerging soon with a new lease on life and a greater inner-standing of who you are as you continue your healing vortex journey.

View this portal less traveled as a deeper layer of consciousness of yourself and of the senses and spirit. You must face hidden memories, concerns, and old stories that lie beneath the surface if you wish to emerge transformed by your experience of the dark night of the soul. Stop and surrender to the universe. The darkest nights are needed to appreciate the light of day. A huge element of moving through existential crisis is shadow work or, as I like to call it—"Shadow WERK." The "WERK" makes it more fun, so just roll with it.

We are all part light and part dark inside. This is a fact of life we must face and embrace. As spiritual beings having a human experience, we have developed two faces. The first face we show the world is our ego or persona. The second face we keep private—it is called the "shadow." In fact, our shadow selves are so private that usually we aren't even aware of their existence.

There is a good reason why our shadows remain locked away within the dark depths of our psyche. Our shadows contain everything considered ugly, bad, shameful, weird, taboo, or socially unacceptable. Our shadows contain the parts of us that were shunned, denied, rejected, or negatively condemned by our parents, family members, and societies while we were growing up. To be loved and accepted, we learned as children to hide away those parts of ourselves that weren't met with praise and approval. Cutting off and burying certain parts of ourselves was a necessary part of our survival. The downside to repressing parts of ourselves is that they begin to fester and can seep out in sabotaging ways. The longer we put off facing our shadows, the more they try to control our lives. If you have ever felt at war with yourself or like your own worst enemy, it is because your shadows are controlling you, not the other way around.

Signs You Have Met Your Shadow

You sense a dark or wounded presence. You feel scared. You feel guilt or shame. You want to run or fight, you may go into denial, or you may want to project onto or blame others. Old memories resurface. You feel angry. You feel tired, weak, or sick to your stomach—just to name a few. It is completely normal to experience any of these feelings or all of them. Please take a break if you get overwhelmed. Then keep going. Every time you confront the shadow self, you create more wholeness and more freedom within your mind, body, and spirit.

What Exactly Is "Shadow WERK"?

You'll occasionally see some people state that Shadow WERK is about "getting in touch with your dark side," which sounds like it's trying to turn you into a Sith Lord like Darth Vader or confront your inner mass murderer or something. That's not it. Nor is it about trying to turn yourself into a being of pure love, positivity, and light. If anything, that would be spiritual bypassing and total avoidance of doing actual Shadow WERK altogether. You shouldn't be burying negative emotions and thoughts or treating them as things to be avoided.

In addition, it's not about shaming people as "beings of darkness" or whatever. No one is accusing you of being Anakin Skywalker. This sounds a *lot* simpler than it is. The reality is that we are all deeply flawed people with our personal baggage. Shadow WERK is about confronting that personal baggage and working on unpacking, putting away, or throwing it out entirely. I'm not going to lie; it's challenging and painful as hell. If you have mental health issues such as PTSD, it's especially painful since you must deal with your triggers head-on. I speak from personal experience here. However, it's a good way to heal from trauma and handle personal growth. You don't need to be traumatized to need to do it. You just need to be human with your own baggage to unpack, and we've all got a few bags that need unpacking, ya dig?

What are some things you don't like about yourself? Why? Where did those behaviors, habits, or traits come from? In what ways are you refusing to change or are resistant to change? (Be honest with yourself; only you will see this.) In what ways are you fighting for control? If the darkest, grittiest part of you was in charge of putting out the dumpster fires in your life, how would it do it? Or did that part of you set the fires? Be honest. How can you embrace your light without embracing your shadow? Take ten to fifteen minutes and journal about your shadow archetypes (the saboteur, the addict, the victim, the complainer, the avoider, and so forth) or any aspect about yourself or others you don't like.

This is a difficult exercise for some, but you might even realize how these shadow parts we play were needed to survive hardship. Perhaps you can release them now or shift them into another, more helpful archetypal energy to support your inner journey. Perhaps there is a role for every part of you. Most importantly, remember that when you are willing to embrace your shadows and shine light on them, you can allow yourself to integrate all parts of yourself with deep compassion; this is a powerful way to feel whole again. Practice saying these healing-vortex-within mantras for embracing your shadow and making that shadow WERK:

"I am going to WERK with my shadow self, not against it."
"I choose to illuminate my shadow to heal and awaken buried treasures within."
"I am creating peaceful solutions within my personality through WERKing and TWERKing my shadow."

CHAPTER 21

The Portal of Luminosity: Light WERK

Sometimes the Universe turns off all the lights so
we have no choice but to find our own.
—Rebecca Campbell

There is a saying that "light workers work in the dark." We have all had experiences in life when things seemed bleak, or we didn't like ourselves or the state of our lives. While learning to WERK with our shadows is an important part of the healing and awakening journey, learning to WERK with our inner light is equally important. We can bring transformation into our lives by using practices I refer to as "Light WERK." Light WERK is essentially the complimentary portal to Shadow WERK. When we open this portal of Light WERK, we can tap back into the things we love about ourselves, the things for which we are grateful, and the things that *light us up* or inspire us. As mentioned previously, inspiration literally translates to "in spirit," and you don't need to be a light worker or a deeply spiritual person to find your light or spark of joy.

Know it or not, we are light beings. Every person can increase their light within and use it to communicate on different planes, heal, and expand consciousness to a fantastic degree. In turn, the light from within us starts to radiate outward from our energy centers, thus affecting the vibrations of those around us. People don't know why, but they start to feel happy and energized, and a feeling of peace may come over them while in your presence. It is a scientific fact that when two energies are brought together, the stronger of the two will alter the other. When you create enough light around you (or positive energy), you will alter the frequencies of the people who share your space, even if they are coarse and negative. It is no mystery why historical books representing spiritual masters always bathed them in light. Light is where knowledge lies. Many people refer to light as information. And within this light is the universal mind completely unfiltered. Information (light) is instantaneous, without words, and of the highest truth.

There are many benefits to Light WERK. If there is friction between you and someone, visualize light between you two. You may find that things then smooth out on their own. If you are about to do something stressful, like a job interview, use light there as well. And of course, you can use light to help you protect your energy and overall health. There are other benefits to Light WERK most don't even realize, including helping the earth in her healing, awakening, and ascension process. The more light or joy we tap into, the more it affects all living things around us. It would be narrow minded to think this doesn't include the very space we live. I have spoken of ascension, and this isn't just for humans but for all sentient life forms. The earth healing and awakening as well as our own doesn't need to be so painful. Through light, we can ease suffering. We change the energy of whatever we send light to, so keep this in mind.

Traveling through the portals of Shadow WERK and Light WERK is a sacred gift you are giving yourself and everyone around you. I highly encourage you to keep a journal where you can regularly jot down the things that inspire you or activate your inner light; these are the people, places, things, experiences, thoughts, feelings, and insights that light you up. Here are some other suggestions to help you activate your portal of Light WERK.

- Draw or visualize your soul's home
- Write down three activities that inspire you and plan to do at least one this week
- Write down three acts of kindness and do them for three people this month
- Journal about an experience that "lit" you up or that inspired you
- Sunbathe or moon bathe

You might not immediately see it, but keeping both a Shadow WERK and a Light WERK journal creates a huge ripple effect in the world, which impacts countless others through your actions. You can WERK and TWERK your shadow and light, and the more conscious you will be of them both. Be proud of yourself for choosing to walk this path. You deserve it. When we are shining our lights brightly in the world, we are honoring who we are, and we often attract wonderful experiences and people too. Just like a lighthouse helping wary sailors find the shore, when we turn on our inner lights, we find our way in life.

Practice using these healing-vortex-within mantras to further support you in tapping into your inner luminosity and beam those lights to WERK:

"I choose to honor my light within and let it guide me."
"I am a clear channel of eternal and luminous light."
"Cosmic light radiates through every cell of my body, and
I awaken the dormant light within me now."

CHAPTER 22

Other People's Portals (OPP)

Our relationships are our greatest teachers.
—Unknown

Life is all about relationships. Relationships are like the connective tissue of life that links us with a wide range of other humans from all walks of life, be it family, friends, coworkers, neighbors, lovers, partners, the gold and silver dude street performers, and even naked bike riders (keep in mind that I lived in San Francisco for twelve years). Each of these relationships has varying dimensions, boundaries, timeframes, intensities, and relationships to sequins or not—if the relationship involves drag queens, of course. We know, as the saying goes, "People come into your life for a reason, a season, or a lifetime." Not every relationship we have will be a healthy one. In fact, many of us have been hurt or traumatized by people we cared about, and this can be one of the many reasons we journey out on our own to embrace the healing and awakening process. In my opinion, no relationship is a waste of time; if a relationship wasn't what you wanted, it showed you what you needed.

Remember that portal chapter about paradoxes? That information most certainly applies to the topic of other people's portals, or OPP, and the relationships we have with so many other souls on this planet of love and chaos. It is incredibly important to remember that everyone is dealing with some form of hardship in their life. Everyone is on some type of healing or awakening journey. Everyone is also at very different stages of this journey and on different paths as well. No one road is better than another, and we want to be aware of this so we don't get sucked into someone's vortex and taken off our own journey. It can be tempting to distract ourselves with other people's portals and other people's problems. We can be supportive and encouraging, but we cannot fix or save another. Having clear and healthy boundaries within your healing vortex for the relationship with yourself will support all other relationships in your life.

We are social creatures, and having a supportive team around us—be it friends, family, or healers of some kind—can profoundly assist us on this journey. Whether it's a shaman, therapist, spirit guide, mentor, coach, or a skilled alternative healer, it is so important to get the support you need and deserve to make all your healing intentions materialize into reality. None of us can do it all alone. Early on in your healing vortex journey, it is incredibly helpful to have a trusted support system of some kind to help you connect, reconnect, and stay connected to your healing goals and higher self. Some people find support online. Others attend groups or seminars or workshops. And others find the support they need through therapy, social or spiritual communities, or other personal connections.

Accessing social support has become increasingly hard during a pandemic, but we are social creatures, and we all need and benefit from aligned connection—even the most introverted "hermity" of hermits of us (speaking from experience). But proceed with caution. I once had a client tell me that "half of all therapists, psychiatrists, and healers are narcissists, and half are empaths." When she shared this insight with me, I got chills down my spine at the heartbreaking reality encompassed in that statement: half of all healing providers are narcissists, and half are empaths. I don't disagree with this statement; while it may be a gross generalization, it does make sense. It struck me as quite accurate, in fact, given some of my horrible experiences accessing therapy and working in the field of mental health for so many years.

I remember this client telling me about a psychiatrist she saw who had said some very inappropriate things in treatment with her and how discouraged and depressed she had gotten following those interactions. It took her a lot to reengage in treatment again, but luckily she didn't give up; and when two fellow empaths work together as equal collaborators, as she and I did, she could have a reparative experience and trust others again. I wish I could say that was the only client who ever shared a traumatic tale with me regarding another provider of some kind, but I hear things like this all too often. It truly breaks my heart when I hear about a client or anyone for that matter being treated unfairly or in an abusive way. I see all my clients and all people as equals, who deserve to be treated with kindness, but unfortunately, many people can mistake our kindness for weakness. For this and many other reasons, please use caution and always trust your intuition when reaching out for support. Just because someone is a doctor or therapist or a person in a position of power or authority, that does *not* mean they are an expert on you or that you should do what they say if it feels wrong to you.

Like me, many of those in the healing professions are empaths and have a deep sense of empathy, giving nature and natural healing abilities. However, some providers are narcissists and they have a superiority complex and simply do the work because it makes them feel good about themselves—not because they care about the client in front of them. This is one reason why the field of psychology has enormous stigma and prevents so many people from getting help. Choose all mental health providers and healers wisely and stay aware of red flags, *especially if you are an empath.* It's truly important that you get the support you need to connect to your inner healer. Even more important is that you trust your intuition about the type of healer/helper who is the best fit for you and find someone who can support you in your independent healing practices—not just take your money forever or make you dependent on them indefinitely.

It is sad but true that not all healers, therapists, and spiritual teachers are of pure intent. Some have ulterior motives, some are burned out, and some just aren't going to align with you. Working in the mental health field and through my personal healing journey, I've seen the darker sides of the healing profession. They have taught me that some healers do more harm than good. I can't tell you how many times I got discouraged along my healing journey before I learned how to be my own healer and began teaching this to others.

Much of the healing work we end up doing for ourselves and others is repairing harm another human has caused. This includes harm caused by a healer. Please do your research and trust your intuition when accessing services; if something feels off or the help you are receiving becomes unhelpful or harmful at any point in time, you must protect yourself. When we accept the fact that our relationships are here to make us conscious instead of happy, then our relationships become a portal for self-mastery that continues to support us on our healing vortex journey.

Practice using these healing-vortex-within mantras to support you in choosing the right OPP and steering clear of the wrong OPP on your healing and awakening journey:

> "I choose to create and maintain healthy relationships with others and myself."
> "I am building a safe and supportive social support network."
> "Everyone is on an inner journey of some kind, and I stay in my healing vortex lane rather than swerve into others."

The Portal to Transmuting Triggers, Trauma, and Tragedy

If tragedy never entered our lives, we wouldn't appreciate the magic.
—Nikki Rowe

We carry trauma in our energy field for up to seven generations back. Therefore, family patterns can be the hardest to break. Often, they aren't even ours to begin with. But we don't know another way to be, so we continue playing out the drama. You are being called to heal your family line or free yourself from living the life of your ancestors. This could mean letting go of an old pattern of your maternal or paternal line. Healing trauma from the past that isn't even yours or observing old ways of being that no longer serve you is what this portal is all about.

The thing to notice when ancestral healing comes up is that you cannot heal another person, but your own healing can cause another person to choose to heal. Energy is freed up. You are being guided now to look at your life and decide how you want it to be. Which ways of being or patterns are you ready to free yourself from? What past, unhelpful trauma narratives do you want to rewrite? What old ways of being from your family line are you ready to let go of? We know that when we start talking about trauma and tragedies, triggers go with the territory.

Triggers suck donkey balls—let's be honest. But I like to call on my inner wizard, or shall I say wizardess, to help me through even the most cataclysmic of triggers. You know why? 'Cause wizards embody the essential archetype of magic and transmutation (among many other extrasensory INNER-G skills). Wizards, mystics, and/or healers are powerful, and they take action. You are powerful too, and you are taking action now by reading this to tap into your inner-transmuting abilities. We all have emotional, mental, physical, and spiritual triggers—yeah, all four, ya dig. It can be challenging to identify what exactly those triggers are, but the process of getting to know and inner-stand them can help us heal and learn how to cope better in response. Why do we all have triggers? Because they are opportunities to heal and awaken. This is what our souls signed up for, remember?

Our souls signed up for this—all of this. All the traumas, losses, painful events, joys, sorrows, hard moments, and duality of the third dimension. We were all children once. When we were growing up, we inevitably experienced pain or suffering we couldn't acknowledge or deal with sufficiently at the time. As adults, we typically become triggered by experiences that are reminiscent of these old, painful feelings.

So, what are *your* triggers? What do you do to manage the painful feelings that are triggered? Do you face your triggers head-on or attempt to avoid the pain? Here are some examples that might help you better identify your triggers:

- Someone rejecting you or you feeling rejected by yourself
- Someone leaving you (or threatening that they will) or you abandoning yourself
- Helplessness over painful situations
- Feeling judged by others, judging others, or judging yourself
- Feeling shame or someone blaming or shaming you
- Someone being too busy to make time for you
- Someone not appearing to be happy to see you
- Someone cutting you off while driving
- Someone trying to control you
- Someone being needy or trying to smother you

Write down your top triggers now and get clear on exactly what they are, when they show up, and what your reactions typically look like. Once you know your triggers, the first step toward healing them is considering their origins. Ask yourself which of your triggers might relate to your childhood experiences. Only you can heal your triggers, but it's normal to want to avoid this messy stuff. It's also typical to avoid our triggers when we are unaware of them. Notice if any of these avoidance techniques relate to you when you are triggered: I get angry. I get needy. I comply. I become a people pleaser. I shut down and withdraw from the other person. I blame someone else for my pain. I turn to an addiction—food, drugs, alcohol, sex, porn, shopping, work, gambling, television, internet, obsessive cleaning, and so on.

If you do relate to any of these responses, how do you feel about them? You'll probably realize that the pain doesn't go away just because you try to avoid it, and you may even end up in more pain ... way more pain. Trust me, I know. I encourage you to be very honest with yourself about your triggers and how you react to them. Even if this approach initially feels harsh, it will help you learn to be more compassionate with yourself. Thinking honestly about your triggers is the only way to eventually heal them.

Inner-Stand What Is beneath Your Triggers

Where there is a trigger (for example, fight, flight, freeze, or fawn response), there is always some kind of pain beneath it. Although we tend to view triggers in a negative light, I have come to learn that the fight, flight, freeze, or fawn response itself is a valid emotional experience, just like happiness or love. And it does, in fact, serve a valid purpose. Triggers send a message to our bodies and brains that something painful within us has been activated and is asking to be acknowledged. In many cases, it signals that there is something much deeper, a wound that brings up vulnerability and pain.

We need to take a step back, go inward, and begin to explore where the triggers for these behaviors and reactions stem from. While growing up, we are conditioned to behave in certain ways based on our environment and circumstances. As children, certain behaviors are ingrained in us by our family and peers. We learn to mimic those around us—for example, how they communicate and respond to one another—and over time we implement those behaviors as our own.

Not only do we mimic their behaviors, but we also take on their fears and beliefs. Then when something triggers these fears and beliefs, we react to protect ourselves. Identifying where these beliefs stemmed from gave me the insight to look at the bigger picture and inner-stand the painful stories I had taken on as my own. It allowed me to take responsibility for my own destructive patterns. I was beginning to see how my reactions were triggered by an unconscious fear out of a need for survival. Your triggers might be completely different, and they may pertain more to pain from your childhood than from inherited beliefs and fears. For example, if your parents regularly shamed you for mistakes when you were a kid, you might react defensively whenever someone points out an area where you have room for improvement. Or if you felt ignored while growing up, you may have a knee-jerk reaction whenever someone can't spend time with you.

The problem is, our conditioning is so deeply ingrained within us that we aren't even aware of our reactions most of the time. They just become an automatic response. We cannot always recognize that we are repeatedly replaying old patterns. We tend to blame external circumstances or others for causing our suffering. When you look back at your past to inner-stand your triggers, it will feel uncomfortable and challenging at times. But when you can sit with your emotions and delve a little deeper, you start breaking through your conditioned patterns and behaviors and set yourself free.

It's important to inner-stand that our conditioning came from many years of reinforcing these old beliefs, so it's no surprise that change won't happen overnight. We need to be kind to ourselves through this process instead of judging ourselves and our mistakes or beating ourselves up if we fall along the way. Each step we take brings us closer to breaking old patterns and forming new, positive ones. So, where to begin? Here are some healing vortex within techniques for breaking old, trauma-induced patterns and portaling to the transmutation station of magic:

Respond Rather Than React

When you experience that old, familiar feeling of anger or frustration bubbling up inside you, don't react. Instead of erupting like a volcano, pouring out hurtful words and reactions, try pausing for a moment. Take some space to reflect and name the emotions that surface—maybe fear, resentment, shame, or desperation—and explore beneath the triggering emotion. Don't try to overanalyze the situation; just sit with the emotions and see what arises. Do you feel vulnerable or powerless? Do you have a sense of sadness, betrayal, or fear?

How Does It Feel in Your Body?

Ask yourself, "Where do these emotions activate in my body? What are the sensations, textures, colors, sounds?" Try to describe the experience like you are a curious wizard looking at something new. The goal here is to observe it rather than to let it become you. Observe rather than absorb. You don't need to like it, but you can accept and observe it for two to three minutes. These sensations are asking for your acknowledgment; send them love.

Identify Your Go-to Response

Ask yourself, "How would I usually respond in this situation?" Maybe you would react by shouting, trying to push someone's buttons, or becoming defensive. Take the time to recognize your usual response and sit with it for a moment. Identify how this response may cause pain and suffering to yourself and others.

Reflect

Ask yourself, "Am I acting from a place of love and kindness?" By asking yourself this, you take the focus off blaming others or the situation. You take responsibility for your own actions and reclaim your personal power. By taking responsibility, you are then able to consciously choose how you respond to any given situation. Remember: you don't have control over how other people respond, but you do have control over your response.

Practice Awareness

Remember: you are acting out a conditioned behavior; it is your automatic response. When you practice awareness by identifying conditioned behaviors, you begin to take the power away from the old patterns and create space to form new, positive ones. It's like rewriting your story. You have the power to recreate your story and transform old patterns into ones that serve you and align with your true essence and purpose in life. Also, be very aware of how much of this energy is yours and how much you may have absorbed from the other person, especially energy vampires. We never want to mirror back those low-vibe frequencies that get thrown at us. Oh no! You can turn shit into sunshine by walking away or responding with kindness. You want to feel good about yourself after the interaction, no matter how the other person behaves.

What Is Beneath the Trigger?

There is the trigger and then there is the core wound beneath the trigger. That is what needs to get looked at and dealt with—trigger wizard style. For example, a person interrupting me when I'm talking might trigger me. However, what is beneath the trigger is that this reminds me of being interrupted often as a child and not feeling heard (in other words, the core wound). Once the core wound beneath the trigger is identified, we can shift into trigger wizard mode.

How do I want to transmute or alchemize this wound into something better? How can I respond—either internally with my self-talk or externally to this person who interrupted me, who is most likely completely unaware of my invisible core wound? What would Merlin do? Personally, I like to make weird lightsaber noises to the chronic interrupter *or* say something like, "Let me finish because it is important to me to know you hear me and inner-stand me, and then I'll be happy to listen to you." I choose to alchemize feeling unheard into speaking up and advocating for myself in ways I was unable to as a child to heal this wound and transmute it into an act of self-love and healthy boundaries. Boom! Trigger wizard magic!

Your conditioned responses and behaviors are your defense mechanisms, the coping strategies you learned to protect yourself in the world. Acknowledge that you've always done your best based on what you learned while growing up, and you're now doing your best to change. You may find it helpful to keep a trigger wizard magicians log (or journal if you want to be basic about it) so you can reflect on the above points when triggers occur, what the underlying core wounds might be, and any old destructive patterns that need a *mega* dose of Merlin Trigger Wizard Magic—or whatever your inner trigger wizard is named.

Transmuting pain into gold and core wounds into self-love has been one of my most reliable healing buddies both professionally with my clients and personally on this healing and awakening journey. I highly recommend that you use a journal or trigger wizard magicians log of some kind to better integrate the healing work you are doing. Additionally, here are some trigger wizard invocations or healing-vortex-within mantras to get the magic flowing:

> "Triggers are opportunities to heal."
> "When I get triggered, I consciously pause, step back, and examine what is beneath the trigger; this is the portal to deeper healing and awakening."
> "I go beyond the trigger portal to my inner vortex of alchemy and magic; I am a trigger wizard!"

CHAPTER 24

The Portal of Feelings

Vulnerability is the portal to feeling. Feeling is the portal to strength.
—A. D. Posey

People allow their feelings to hold them captive. They spend much of their lives resisting their true feelings. Guilt makes them lament, anger makes them feel guilty, sadness makes them feel weak, and hate makes them feel scared. Some people choose to numb these feelings with alcohol, drugs, or sex, while some try to suppress them by exerting extreme control over their emotions. The numbing down or controlling of your feelings and emotions works for a while, but then it hits you, hits you hard. If we numb the pain, we will never know if we are healing, so you got to feel it to heal it. And this is probably the best advice to anyone who hates the feelings that make them vulnerable.

How often do we deny our feelings or not allow ourselves to feel something? How often do we use drugs, alcohol, shopping, TV, or other empty distractions to numb or divert away from difficult emotional experiences? Feeling our feelings is extremely hard at times. Pushing feelings away and not being honest with ourselves about emotions only intensifies and delays the healing process. If you keep sweeping dirt under the rug, eventually there is a mountain of dirt that debilitates you.

You've got to feel it to heal it. This isn't just a cute saying that rhymes. Allow yourself to feel your feelings. You don't need to stay in that emotional experience forever. Nothing lasts forever. Feelings come and go. The more you allow the feelings to come, the easier you can let them go and improve the flow of your spirit in the healing vortex within and all around you as well, like a revolving door easily moving emotional energy in and out. The more you allow yourself to feel, the more fulfilling your healing journey and personal growth will be.

When life brings some crazy situation in the form of the demise of a loved one or some childhood trauma or failed career or relationship, we are unable to face the real pain that comes with it, so we look for ways to escape it. But the only way out is through it. If therapy or any form of self-work is to be effective, it must go directly to the source of the pain and the feelings. We must be willing to go inward and visit the places we don't want to go. We must learn how to keep company with all our emotions, not just the ones we like to feel. We must make a practice of tuning into our internal experience and asking ourselves difficult questions: What am I trying to keep myself from feeling? Do I think it isn't okay to feel my feelings and why? How can I practice soul-*full* self-care around my feelings and that trigger wizard stuff too to avoid getting stuck in them? Remember: the healing and awakening journey isn't linear. They are interdependent and a supportive tapestry of resources to continue to travel through. No feeling is final, and your inner journey now has dozens of tools so you don't get stuck in any emotional quicksand. You just need to remember to use them.

When you feel bad, it's natural to want to feel better; but once you start practicing this stuff, you'll never again want to settle for feeling better when you know you can get better. You are capable, and you are worth it. It's not that hard once you do it for a minute or two, and then you won't explode like a dumpster fire volcano on people you love. Emotional self-mastery begins by feeling your feelings and not avoiding them, and I know you are well on the way to being an emotional self-mastery badass after this powerful portal. Place one hand on your heart and one hand on your stomach as you breathe slowly, saying these healing-vortex-within mantras:

> "It is safe to feel my feelings."
> "Emotional pain will not kill me, but running from it can."
> "I allow myself to feel; I allow myself to release and heal."

CHAPTER 25

The Prison Break Portal: Free Your Mind and the World

Free your mind and the rest will follow.
—En Vogue

Not only is it a catchy line from an En Vogue song, but the title of this chapter is truly words to live by. Are you truly a free sovereign being if you are plagued by thoughts that imprison you in your body? When we constantly replay in our minds events and people who harmed us and cheated us or incidents that upset us and made us angry, we get locked in a negative loop. Like a bad TV show, we relive those feelings again and again. These recurring thought patterns are toxic to us both physically and mentally.

Toxic thoughts, negative emotions, and worry and negative self-talk affect us at a biological level and affects how our immune cells talk to each other. They also directly affect how well they can fight off invaders like viruses that cause colds and flu. Believe it or not, but something as seemingly unrelated as negative self-talk and negative thoughts could harm your immune system. Unfortunately, no one talks about this when you go to the doctor for a checkup.

The fact is, negativity can make you physically ill. This is because negative thinking, worry, and fear-based thinking change your brain. They signal the brain to release stress hormones (chemical messengers) to put your entire body in high alert to cope with the perceived danger. The brain diverts resources from the immune system that weaken your immune cells, causing inflammation in various parts of the body. The first step to stopping this vicious cycle is to acknowledge it is an issue for you. Once you have accepted this link between mind and body, you can convince your brain to act to stop it. We may not realize it, but negative feelings can be as toxic to our health as physical poisons, wearing on us and causing depression, illness, and burnout.

If your mind, body, and soul were trapped in a prison, wouldn't you want to set them free? The good news is, you are both the prisoner and the prison guard. You are both the warden and the parole board. Remember the paradox portal. While we aren't always responsible for the pain or trauma inflicted on us, we are absolutely 100 percent responsible for healing it and freeing ourselves from toxic thoughts, mind control schemes, poisonous foods, chemicals, and a lack of spiritual alignment. You keep your mind locked up in those toxic thoughts every time your inner critic is allowed to drive the bus.

The average person has sixty thousand to seventy thousand thoughts a day. That's a lot of neural signals firing, baby! *Pew, pew, pew pew* (remember that's the sound they make ;-). And the vast majority of those thoughts are negative, even on a good day. Our brains are hardwired for survival, and our brains love to problem solve. The negative, automatic thoughts that pop up on repeat in the background like elevator music are there for us all. What matters the most are the thoughts you consciously choose to tell yourself and the mantras you choose to say aloud to rewire your brain and break out of the prison brain cell. One or two conscious and deliberate thoughts or mantras a day can counterbalance thousands of negative, automatic filler thoughts.

Even more good news about all that gray matter in our skulls is that our brains have wondrous neuroplasticity. Neuroplasticity is basically a fancy way of saying our brains are highly trainable, just like a brand-new puppy. The brain's capacity to continue growing and evolving in response to life experience is exactly what this book and your journey in life is all about. Scientists used to believe the brain stopped growing after childhood, but more recent research has shown that the brain continues to refine its architecture over time. This is a truly important discovery, so thank you, brain scientists. The brain's neuroplasticity means it's possible to change negative thinking and behaving patterns and to develop new mindsets, memories, skills, abilities, and *attitudes!* Somebody better call Patti LaBelle, because we *all* need a new attitude.

So, what kind of brain architecture do you want to build with your new attitude? Do you want to keep building prison industrial complexes, or would you rather build a magical oasis sanctuary with lush gardens, constantly blooming flowers, a soul train unicorn orchestra, and a slam poetry roller coaster? That's what my brain architecture looks like, but yours most likely looks different. Why not start building these new brain pathways to it now? Sure, it will take some time to learn a few new skills to ensure what you build in your brain has a strong foundation. I mean, no one picks up the guitar and just starts shredding like Slash from Guns N' Roses. It takes a little practice, but if it means you can break free from a mental prison and toxic thought patterns and behaviors, and develop mental self-mastery, do you think it's worth a try?

Want the blueprint and keys to tunnel out of the mental prison you keep getting locked up in *and* all the materials to build your perfect brain architecture neuroplastic dream home? Practice saying these healing-vortex-within mantras and break free now ... or at least start to tunnel out. Remember: you can always change a thought, *and* if you change your thoughts, you can change the whole world.

> "I consciously create harmonious thoughts that help me and the world."
>
> "I am the master of my own mind; I choose to free myself from imprisoning thoughts."
>
> "I am building new neural pathways by choosing different thoughts; I am building a better, more beautiful internal world now."

CHAPTER 26

Reality Check Portal: There Is Nothing Wrong with You!

Most people don't really want the truth. They just
want constant reassurance that what they believe is the
truth. In other words, cognitive dissonance.
—Dr. Raymond Nichols

***Disclaimer alert on this portal: it might be very triggering or confronting for some of you—so please go slowly and travel back to previous chapters, if needed, to transmute the triggers or practice soul-*full* self-care. Come back when you are ready to confront this deeply transformative, though challenging portal on your healing and awakening journey.

Reality check: *Cognitive dissonance is at the core of many problems both individually and collectively.* Cognitive dissonance is the discomfort experienced when two cognitions (thoughts, attitudes, personal values, or behaviors) are incompatible with each other. Cognitive dissonance is the unpleasant mental state that often results when someone has certain beliefs but acts in a way that contradicts them. A person who experiences this internal inconsistency tends to become psychologically uncomfortable (and often physically, spiritually, and energetically uncomfortable too), and they tend to justify the stressful behavior by using defense mechanisms of rationalizing or avoiding circumstances and contradictory information. Cognitive dissonance often creates inconsistency leading to mental anguish and suffering. It is hard as fuck to be brutally honest with ourselves and look at the hard truths in the world. Some people will inevitably resolve cognitive dissonance by blindly believing whatever they want to believe despite the facts or contradictions in their lives.

Cognitive dissonance is more prevalent than we might realize. It is present in both the smallest, simplest examples to the deepest layers of humanity, which impact the way we interact with each other and view ourselves and the entire universe. Examples of cognitive dissonance include, but are not limited to, the following:

- Meat eating (you believe in animal rights yet justify eating meat for nutrition or cultural reasons)
- Smoking (you know it can cause cancer but justify that you don't smoke enough to do harm)
- Avoiding unpleasant or traumatic medical procedures (you are told by people in positions of authority and/or trust your doctor's advice to get said procedure, yet intuitively or morally you disagree with the harm it may cause)
- Cheating (everyone knows it's wrong, yet so many people cheat on their partners or spouses)
- Not picking up after your dog (you know you shouldn't leave that giant dog turd on Mrs. Conner's lawn, but you forgot the poop bags and/or just don't feel like picking up shit today)
- Being unproductive at work (you have plenty to do and value your job, yet you seem to find yourself online watching cat videos instead of getting anything done)
- Not exercising (you value your health and joined a gym, but you haven't been there once in a year)
- And the list goes on and on in both big and small ways

Since cognitive dissonance creates inconsistency, it can lead to mild to severe discomfort. You become motivated to return to a place of harmony by doing one of three things: (1) change your beliefs, (2) change your actions, or (3) change how you viewed your actions. The more aware you are of this pattern of cognitive dissonance in us *all,* the more you're able to inner-stand yourself on a deeper level and explore what values, morals, attitudes, actions, and beliefs truly matter to you in both the short and long-term healing and awakening journey. And please don't be too hard on yourself when you recognize the process of cognitive dissonance has occurred in your life.

The truth is, there's nothing wrong with you. You live in a world that told you there was something wrong with you since you were born, and that is the real issue—which brings me to my next very important reality check in this powerful portal chapter. *There is nothing wrong with you, and most importantly, you are not your diagnosis.*

People of the world, please do me a favor and *stop* diagnosing yourself online. Seriously, I love you, but please stop trying to diagnose yourself after watching a sixty-second TikTok video or seeing a very convincing TV commercial that you need medication or even reading an article online from a reliable source. One of the greatest problems in this world is that people are so busy trying to find a label or diagnosis for issues we all have. Yes, some people suffer from "clinical" diagnoses, but those must be diagnosed by a qualified provider who specializes in the area they are concerned about. All too often I see people lean on their diagnosis to explain who they are. And all too often, this creates a complacent mentality of blaming the diagnosis rather than doing the work to overcome the root cause.

You are not your diagnosis! No one walks up to someone for the first time and introduces themselves by saying, "Hi, I'm depressed. Nice to meet you" or "Hi, I'm a perfectionist with a fear of intimacy." Yet too many people wear their diagnosis like a badge of victim glorification and an excuse not to be accountable for their lives and their healing journey.

What does a diagnosis actually mean? *Dia* means "going through, across, or between." *Gnosis* means "knowledge of spiritual mysteries and awareness of spiritual knowledge or insight into humanity's real nature as divine." Therefore, the word *diagnosis* translates to going through or in between the process of spiritual knowledge and awareness. *Boom!* A diagnosis is so much more than a label or a cluster of symptoms, for which you may or may not meet the criteria. It is literally a portal leading to the deliverance of the divine spark within humanity from the constraints of earthly existence. Moving through a diagnosis frees you from the constraints of the wound and limits of the third dimension. It is a tool for deeper inner-standing; it isn't who you are.

Therapy can be a useful catalyst for many people to heal. However, the field of mental health, psychology, psychiatry, and modern Western medicine generally treats only the symptoms. To truly and deeply heal from the source of all issues, we need to address the core root of why and where the problem initially began. For example, to treat a cavity, a person will go to the dentist to get that tooth filled, or he or she may even need a crown or a root canal. *But* ... to stop getting cavities and heal what is at the root cause, a person might need to stop eating sugar, might need to brush and floss their teeth more regularly, or might make other lifestyle changes. Another example commonly seen in therapy sessions is when a client comes in for support with anxiety, but the root of the issue is trauma. We can treat the symptoms of anxiety so the client hopefully doesn't keep having panic attacks, but to heal the root cause of the anxiety, we need to address the childhood trauma, attachment issues, avoidance, and other maladaptive coping strategies that have developed to truly support deeper healing and awakening.

There are many ways to heal and shift our consciousness, especially when we address the root or the core wound—and often doing so doesn't even involve talking to a therapist or healer for years about the same issues. We can talk for hours about our problems. The truth is that our greatest addiction is talking about what's negative, thinking about what's negative, and giving energy to what we don't want. Yes, therapy is helpful, especially when it combines practical tools and skills and depth and energy work. This type of therapy can be hard to find; that's why I've written this book. I think the world of mental health, psychology, and Western medicine in general needs a complete makeover, redo, and paradigm shift. Let's take our power back and activate our inner healing magic instead of giving them away or shutting them down completely.

Use these healing-vortex-within mantras to further reality check your life:

> "I am safe and loved and grounded; I can change my thoughts and behaviors and shift dissonant energy."
> "I am not my diagnosis; a diagnosis is simply a portal to deeper awareness and inner-standing."
> "There is *nothing* wrong with me! I am free from self-limiting beliefs."

CHAPTER 27

The Hidden Portals of Healing and Awakening

We can make ourselves miserable, or we can make
ourselves strong. The amount of effort is the same.
—Pema Chodran

I don't suffer from insanity. I enjoy every minute of it.
—Unknown

This is one of my favorite portals of healing and awakening because sometimes, when you least expect it, you stumble upon a hidden portal of healing and awakening you didn't even know existed. This happened for me one foggy San Francisco night when I met my neighbor, a friend of over ten years, the legendary Dog Man of San Francisco, James (and his three dogs). This is one of my favorite memories of my twelve years of living in San Francisco's Wharf Beach District; that's what I dubbed it at least. For those of you who aren't familiar with Wharf Beach, it is a micro neighborhood located between North Beach and Fisherman's Wharf, often referred to as North North Beach. It was my triple OG stomping grounds, and this story is a classic tale of how magically weird and healing the city of San Francisco is.

I had been out that Saturday night to see a few of my friends, who were working at various bars across the city, before going to one of my favorite clubs to see my favorite DJ, Mark Farina. It was a great show, but about halfway into it, a drunk damsel in distress vomited all over me in the bathroom. I did my best to clean both of us up, but it was a time-to-fucking-go moment since my glittery, sequined, and fur ensemble was soggy and smelly beyond repair. The drunk damsel found her group of friends, and they took off in their car as I waved down the nearest taxi and zoomed home. I couldn't even bring myself to enter my apartment in what I was wearing, so I stripped down to my undies and tossed the pile of soggy, sequined, puke-coated clothes down the trash chute and safely dipped into my lair. Sigh. What a bummer! I decided that rather than letting what had happened ruin my evening, I was going to shower and put on my favorite, most comfy unicorn onesie and romp around my neighborhood.

As silly as it sounds, one of my favorite things to do is to stand on the corner of Stockton and Bay Streets in a unicorn onesie while yelling, "Pickles!" into the foggy night air. It is cathartic and weird and deeply symbolic of who I am. And I do my best to be unapologetically me as much of the time as possible. That time of night, after all the tourists have left, is often deserted and eerily peaceful. As I was prancing around in my unicorn comfy fit, having a salty pickle vocal release, I heard someone in the distance yell, "Pickles!" as well. *Who could this pickled twin in the night be?* I thought as I looked down my block to see a man in a Dalmatian dog onesie with two little Chihuahuas on a leash. As we both yelled, "Pickles!" in unison and made eye contact, we also laughed in unison at our similar apparel choices.

"Hey, dude, that's my line," I said jokingly as he approached my corner of the block.

"Love the onesie! I lost my dog Pickles, and I'm trying to find her," he replied.

"You look very familiar," I said as he replied, "I'm James, the Dog Man of San Francisco. I live around the corner. Nice to meet a neighbor who loves onesies too!" And it was certainly nice to have a neighbor friend who appreciated pickles and onesies indeed.

I helped James find his dog Pickles, who had gotten off her leash, as he introduced me to his other two dogs, Einstein and Arnold Schwarzenegger. We ended up chatting for a couple of hours on the streets of good ole Wharf Beach about all kinds of deep, meaningful topics; and it restored my faith in humanity during a time in my life where the only real interactions I was having with people were at work or getting puked on in dark disco clubs by myself. James ended up being one of the few consistent people in my life for years as my neighbor—a deep conversationalist and a lover of animals, pickles, and onesies. Not only was this such a magical, hidden portal of healing, but it was also an example of when OPP (other people's portals) collide with ours for the greater good of both. You never know when you might have an experience like this and weren't even expecting it. Hidden portals of healing and awakening are all around us. When you change the way you look at life, every day and interaction you have with people could be a hidden portal of healing and awakening—and you don't need to be puked on to find them either.

You're being called into this hidden portal of healing and awakening to energetically scan your life for things that may no longer be a vibrational match for who you are and how you've grown, to dismantle the systems and ways of being that once served you and others but no longer do so, and to recognize what makes you happy, what lights you up no matter how weird or esoteric it may be—even if it involves onesies and yelling, "Pickles!" Find and follow your bliss. When you shine your weird light brightly into the night, other weirdos find you like a glittery unicorn lighthouse made of pickles and friendship.

I realized that night that going to clubs and bars wasn't in alignment for me anymore, and I wanted to connect with more people on deeper levels. Sure, I still went to a show here and there or to say hi to my favorite friends when they were working at a local watering hole or karaoke bar, but just being aware of what was in alignment for me and what wasn't allowed me to attract more people like James into my life—more authentic, old souls who can see beyond the veil.

Some of us are here to lift the veil between the seen and unseen worlds, to shine a light on things that are inauthentic or unaligned with the survival and well-being of earth, to stand for and protect those who don't have a voice, and to look deeper and question everything previous generations didn't. We are here to bring society and humanity back into harmony with the planet and the creator at large. If we tolerate things in our lives that aren't aligned and congruent with it, we add to the misalignment of the planet. You're being called to trust yourself; notice what's out of alignment. Notice distortions and lies within the world at large and then take the steps required to bring it back into harmony. Notice what your soul feels called to do and say and yes, even wear. Trust that what lights you up will light your way and that there are so many magical and hidden portals of healing everywhere in every way across every day if you choose to see them that way. Oooo, that rhymed. This is no easy feat, but it's so worthwhile, both individually and for the planet. Take a moment and ask yourself, what are some hidden portals of healing I have encountered recently? How can you stay more open to the hidden realms of healing and awakening in everyday life?

Use these healing-vortex-within mantras to support you in traveling down the hidden portals of healing and awakening anytime you want to see beyond the veil:

> "I choose to stay in alignment with my soul and the hidden realms of healing."
>
> "I am aware of and open to the hidden portals of healing and awakening that happen every day."
>
> "I shine my weird light bright so other weirdos know where to find me."

CHAPTER 28

The Portal of Electric Inner Child WERK

I believe that this neglected, wounded inner child of
the past is the main source of human misery.
—John Bradshaw

The most potent muse of all is our own inner child.
—Steven Nachmanovictch

No matter how big or small, all of us experienced core wounding or trauma as children. These traumas could vary from having your favorite stuffed toy thrown in the trash to being abandoned by your best childhood friend, to being physically or emotionally abused by your parents. Many of us learn to bury or repress these wounds and trauma and/or develop unhealthy coping mechanisms with the limited resources we have when we are kids. Most kids, in an attempt to understand these wounds and traumas, internalize them. Unhelpful, internalized beliefs include, "I must be a bad kid" or "I must not be good enough or lovable." As we carry this buried pain into adulthood, we often experience similar dynamics in our lives and relationships. That subconscious is a sneaky thing trying to get us to heal and awaken even without our awareness. There is a saying that we don't have relationship problems; we have childhood problems disguised as relationship problems. So what do we do about them? The answer is inner child WERK but as I like to do things … with a twist … an electric twist.

Inner child work is the process of contacting, inner-standing, embracing, and healing your inner child. Your inner child represents your first original self that entered this world; it contains your capacity to experience wonder, joy, innocence, sensitivity, and playfulness. Unfortunately, we live in a society that forces us to repress our inner child and "grow up." But the truth is that while most adults are physically "grown up," they never quite reach emotional or psychological adulthood. In other words, most grown-ups aren't adults at all. When we deny and snuff out the voice of the child within, we accumulate heavy psychological baggage. This unexplored and unresolved baggage causes us to experience problems such as mental health issues, physical ailments, and relationship dysfunction. In fact, it could be said that the lack of conscious relatedness to our own inner child is one of the major causes of the severe issues we see today in the world. From the brutal way we treat the environment to the cruel way we talk to ourselves, we have become completely separated from our original innocence.

Your inner child is the part in your subconscious mind that still retains its innocence, creativity, innate magical gifts, and wonder toward life. Your inner child is the metaphorical child that lives within you—within your psyche, within your mind, and within your soul. Your inner child represents the original "you" or the essence that entered this world. The child archetype is a Jungian archetype, first suggested by Carl Jung. In more recent years, many different sub-archetypes of the inner child have been suggested too, such as "wounded child," "abandoned or orphan child," "dependent child," "magical or innocent child," "nature child," "divine child," and "eternal child."

There are many types of child archetypes, and I will outline them here so you can get a sense of yours. The mature child archetype is the part of us that nurtures us and is lighthearted and innocent; it watches for the wonders of the world, no matter what age we might be. It brings playfulness and balance to our lives and brings out the best in others. The wounded child archetype is often fixated on the abuse, neglect, and traumas that were experienced in childhood and often blame their parents for challenges in their life and relationships. Since therapy has become more acceptable, many people identify with this archetype. The positive side of the wounded child is that they have the desire to help other wounded children and have a deep ability to be compassionate.

Those with the orphan child archetype don't feel they belong to their families and often become independent early and feel like they raised themselves and may experience feelings of abandonment. Those with the magical child archetype see beauty in all things. They maintain wisdom and courage when what is happening around them may be catastrophic. Pessimism and depression can surface, especially if the magical child had a dream adults discouraged. The eternal child archetype manifests as an ability to stay young in body, mind, and spirit. These children continue to have fun and enjoy life, even as they age, but they can have an inability to grow up and be responsible or live outside the conventional norm of adulthood and remain childlike, not taking on the responsibilities of the adult.

A New and Unique Archetype: The Electric Inner Child

The Electric Inner Child archetype encompasses a mix of qualities from the Indigo, Crystal, and Rainbow Children archetypes. Indigo Children generally exhibit the following characteristics:

- They were born between the 1960s and the 1990s
- They are rebellious and warrior in spirit
- They despise the system
- They love to isolate themselves
- They are prone to addictions and are stubborn
- They want to rage against the corrupted system that governs society, and this trait projects itself in the art, music, movies, movements, and lifestyles of their youth
- They may have experimented with psychedelic substances, and they forced their minds to be open for spiritual or existential awakenings

All these qualities contributed to the creation of new businesses and inventions, like the internet, that changed the future forever. How does the Indigo Child archetype show up in you? Record your reflections.

Crystal Children are most likely to be born from the people of Generation X. Gen Xers were typically born between 1960 and 1979, and they may identify as Indigos, though these archetypal star children can be born at any interval of time. Crystal Children generally fall into the Generation Y category since they are usually born between 1980 and

2000 (also commonly known as "millennials"). Crystal children generally exhibit the following characteristics:

- They are strong and pure-hearted
- They have highly developed imaginations and creativity
- They are extremely empathetic and emotional
- They are passionate about supernatural phenomena and superheroes
- They are easygoing
- They are intuitive
- They are born during a transition time, in a period when humanity made its biggest leap in technological advancement, which affected all areas of society
- They grew up in times without the internet and times when they cannot imagine how they lived without the internet

This transition happened in only a ten-year period, which is such a small amount of time for such a great change. This affected their way of seeing the world. It's like they were forced to raise their consciousness at an accelerated rate. Their art, music, movies, businesses, and lifestyles are inspired and driven by various superheroes they idolized while they were growing up. How does the Crystal Child archetype show up in you? Record your reflections.

Rainbow Children are the newest generation of people, or Generation Z, born after the new millennium. They are modern and more technologically advanced than Generation X and Y because they are raised in a period when humans are more connected than at any time in known human history. They had all the information in the world available to them while they were growing up by only pushing a few buttons. These kids are happy and positive. They are like a breath of fresh air. They are bringing happiness and joy to the whole world through various inventions, platforms, and mediums Generation X developed and Generation Y perfected. Rainbow Children generally have the following traits:

- They were born after the new millennium
- They are technologically advanced, and they easily understand new gadgets

- They are loving and hard to contain
- They love animals and nature
- They are possibly vegan
- They are free spirited and often free of karmic wounds the previous two types have (in other words, freer souls)

Their light and positivity make them freer than any generation in modern history. Think of them like light; they give warmth and life, and they cannot be captured. Their whole being is pure, and that's why most of these kids are vegan. How does the Rainbow Child archetype show up in you? Record your reflections.

The greatest differences between Indigos, Crystals, and Rainbow Children archetypes are as follows: The Indigos are here to destroy what's not working and pave the way for a better world. The Crystals are the ones who need to create, develop, and build the new way, uniting the best from the old and the new. The Rainbow Children are here to give life and fertilize the new and improved world, which is in harmony with nature and human potential. All three of these divine inner child archetypes need to work together so there will be a real change to the way humanity further develops—hence the creation of the Electric Inner Child archetype.

The Electric Inner Child is a harmonious blend of all three of the above. The Electric Child is alive and well within us all, and we need to tap into this powerful force to heal ourselves, our ancestral lineages, our current relationships, and the collective. The Electric Inner Child is how we are all part of this spiritual revolution: we are all connected to one another. The spiritual revolution begins within each of us. This spiritual revolution is a consequence of the collective human psyche. To inner-stand this, we must over-stand how we are all connected. We must grasp the fact that *everything* connects to everything else, even our thoughts. As the truest and most authentic expression of your essence, your inner child carries tremendous wisdom and profound pain.

How does the Electric Inner Child archetype show up in you? Extrapolate the most desired qualities from the Indigo, Crystal, and Rainbow Child (previously listed above) that you want to embody in your healing vortex journey. How can you apply these characteristics to help yourself and others in your daily life?

How can we finally break the circle of suffering and feel alive and *electric* again? The answer is through the sacred process of Electric Inner Child WERK. Electric Inner Child WERK is revolutionary in that it goes directly to the root of our pain—the pain that started in childhood.

Electric Inner Child WERK empowers us to dig deep, unearth our original wounds, face and feel our pain, and experience life through new eyes.

When you start doing Electric Inner Child WERK, you will begin feeling more resilient, creative, energetic, spontaneous, blissful, hopeful, loving, and more deeply connected with your heart and soul. Above all, please know that this work is deep work that has profound implications for the whole of society. By doing this inner work, you are not only helping yourself but also sending out ripples of change that will influence the whole of humanity as we know it. What you are doing is sacred work, and the impacts are very real.

If you haven't consciously connected with your inner child before, it's important that you know what to expect. Please inner-stand that everyone reacts similarly when first doing this work. To empower you with knowledge and perspective, and to help you feel a sense of safety, here are some common signs that you've touched your inner child and deeper childhood issues while progressing through this healing portal:

- You feel grief and/or deep sadness
- You feel sick to your stomach
- You feel profound joy and/or relief or release of stagnant energies
- You feel hypersensitive or fragile
- You want to address past hurts with your family
- You feel overwhelming emotions
- You feel deeply compassionate toward yourself.
- You want to scream at life
- You feel tired or weak
- You feel ashamed
- You feel excited about life and become more open to embracing change

Please know that it's normal to experience all of these. Please be patient and gentle with yourself, walk away when needed, practice self-love, and set healthy boundaries for yourself and others. If, at any point, you feel inundated with painful emotions, please walk away and revisit the self-care portal. Then keep going. With every step, you are creating more healing, more wholeness, and more freedom within your entire being.

As a loving warning, I want to emphasize that this portal isn't a replacement for therapy or psychological help. If you suffer from a history of extreme abuse or trauma, please seek out professional guidance first and use this portal and book as a supplement for your healing journey. Second, if you are struggling with an addiction or have severe mental health impairments, please do not attempt the activities within this portal chapter until you are more stable. Third, if at any time a disturbing memory resurfaces or you feel inundated by strong emotions, please stop. Take a break. Practice self-care. And if necessary, seek out professional help, particularly if you've had a memory of being abused in some way.

Simple Ways to Connect with Your Inner Child and Become Electric

Speak to Your Inner Child—Acknowledge your inner child and let it know you're there for it. Treat it with kindness and respect. Some self-nurturing things you could say to your inner child, for example, include, "I love you. I hear you. I see you. I'm sorry. Thank you for being you. I forgive you. You are a wonderful, beautiful soul, and I am going to protect you now." Make a habit of talking to your inner child. You could also communicate through journal work by asking your inner child a question, then writing down the response.

Look at Pictures of Yourself as a Child—Go through old photo albums and rediscover what your younger self looked like. Let that image be burned into your brain, because it will serve you well throughout the rest of your inner child work. You might even like to put photos of yourself next to your bedside table, in your wallet, or around the house just to remind yourself of your inner child's presence.

Recreate What You Loved to Do as a Child—Sit down and think about what you loved to do as a child. Maybe you liked climbing trees, playing with toy blocks, cuddling toy bears, or eating warm porridge. Maybe you wanted to be Goldilocks as a kid. I know I did. Make time to include whatever activity you loved to do as a child in your present life. As silly as this seems, it is self-care and self-love for your inner child.

Create an Inner-Child Altar—This is my favorite, and I have one in my home office that I often meditate in front of, bring treats to, and charge my healing crystals with when I do inner child healings for me and my clients. I have a few of my favorite pictures of me at various ages, two My Little Ponies I found in my mom's hall closet (that she saved for me not too long ago), candles, and a few cherished crystals.

Commit to do at least one small thing every week to honor your inner child. The importance of play, silliness, and honoring our inner child is sadly undervalued as adults, but that needs to change. We need more fun, love, and play in the world. We need more people tapping into their inner child so the souls who are still children and the new souls becoming children every day are deeply protected and treated and honored with more love. Through Inner Child WERK, people have told me that they've connected to sides of themselves they never even knew existed as adults. This discovery is truly life changing. It's important that you make a habit of this "playtime" and explore any embarrassment or silliness you feel toward it. It's completely normal to feel a bit foolish at first, but it's important to keep an open mind. In addition, you can practice using these healing-vortex-within mantras to honor your inner child:

> "My inner child is the portal to joy and laughter and feeling alive again."
> "Nurturing my Electric Inner Child is a powerful portal to health, healing, and awakening."
> "The more I love and care for my inner child, the more I have access to the electric energy to heal myself and improve the world."

CHAPTER 29

The Portal of Incension (The Inner Ascension)

Incension is the return to the source of eternal life through
the inner planes of our own being, polarity integration,
and direct union with the source of all life.
—Zarina Avatara Anada

People talk a lot about "ascension" in various spiritual and religious communities and in healing and awakening practices. Ascension is the act of rising to a higher level. This can mean many things in your current lifetime and beyond. While *ascension* is often used as a religious or spiritual word, it also deeply applies to the healing journey and ascending through the portals in this book to reach a higher level of consciousness and self-mastery. *Incension* is a more accurate word for the healing journey, because *incension* means going within to ascend, awaken, and/or heal, which is exactly what we are doing in this book and beyond.

The layers and complexities that exist with the fields of quantum physics and other sciences, combined with the often contradictory or false light information in the spiritual communities, can be confusing and often turn people off from diving deeper into these areas. My goal is to keep things as simple as possible while also giving my readers practical tools and information to empower their inner journey.

We are in a very profound time on earth when densities or dimensions are shifting. We have all felt it in some way or another. Many traditional religious dogmas speak of ascension as a physical transition to "heaven" or the afterlife. The inner ascension or incension I am referring to in this portal has little to do with your flesh prison or other aspects of your physical existence, although our consciousness does affect our physical form. Dimensions can be thought of as states of consciousness. Once we work with dimensions beyond the third, they aren't physical. Just think of where you go on the astral plane or the fourth dimension of time and the dream realm. The fifth dimension so many refer to isn't a physical place; it is a state of consciousness that requires you to raise your energetic frequency within to get there (a.k.a. incension).

Your energetic field is in a state of change and expansion by this stage of the healing and awakening adventure. You have begun to vibrate at higher levels as your consciousness moves more in alignment with your higher self, the best version of you. You are now a forerunner working toward incension to raise the consciousness of this planet. The changes you are experiencing are not always comfortable, but they are necessary for your continued growth. The true beauty of your soul is beginning to show, and it has a positive and uplifting effect on others. There's always another level up. There's always another layer or realm to explore—more grace, more light, more generosity, more compassion, more to release, more to grow, more to love.

We know everything in the universe consists of energy in a continual state of motion. Good old physics taught us that. We are energy beings of light and sound at the fundamental core of our cells, continually creating, recycling, adapting, and changing to the environments we interact with. We are in a density or dimensional shift where thick layers of distortion and pathologies are being dislodged from multiple facets of our being. We can blame the external for everything, avoid facing our own consumption, and deny our divinity and sovereignty; or we can be self-accountable, fiercely face every way we have participated in schemes to get love or validation or comfort, and fully embrace the *incension*—the inner ascension now.

Place both hands on your heart and breathe deeply into the core of your soul as you repeat these healing-vortex-within mantras:

> "I am now ready to move forward and shift into a higher
> level of consciousness within."
> "I am shifting my focus on the external and going within
> the portal of my soul."
> "I go within for all need and desire."

CHAPTER 30

The F-Word Portals

There are no other f-words that offend people
more than *fear* and *forgiveness.*
—Dr. Heather

Fear and forgiveness are very intertwined. These two experiences of fear and forgiveness often debilitate us and create distress and disease, but when we combine them for the highest good on our healing and awakening journey, they become powerful portals that transport us to mend what is broken within. Have you ever broken a bone? Once healed, the place of the break becomes the strongest part of the bone. Our minds, hearts, and souls are the same. We forget that treating the body as some separate machine from the invisible forces within us works against a holistic or whole-person approach to healing and awakening. And I'm a whole-person kinda hoe for healing and awakening.

When you are unwell or in disease, it's too easy to berate yourself for not healing. Healing is a process, and part of that process involves forgiveness. Forgiveness is fucking hard; it's a real f-word. If you are having trouble with forgiveness, you can't afford to be hard on yourself for not being able to let go. You must stop berating yourself for not being able to let go or forgive. You undermine your healing process when you continue to pick on yourself. It is difficult to thrive, let alone heal, when you are being bullied. Bullying yourself isn't the answer. Each time you berate yourself, you throw one more obstacle in the way of your powerful and unique healing vortex journey.

In a world that promotes instant gratification, speedy service, and fast deliveries, many have been led to believe that quick and instant fixes are not only possible but also expected. It is too easy to transfer and apply this notion to healing, but by doing so, you are led to expect an immediate cure. It is tempting to go on a never-ending search for miracle treatments and cures instead of concentrating on genuine ways to better manage your situation.

Many health problems develop over a period, so it takes time to undo them. They often develop due to deficiencies and/or excesses of things that are good or bad for your health, so it also takes energy to undo. Your energy needs to be returned to a balanced state of being. Excesses need to be reduced, and deficiencies need to be filled up again. With time and energy on your side, you improve your chances of creating better health.

There is rarely an instant fix to correct the damage to health—especially mental, emotional, and spiritual health. It takes a series of steps and stages of adjustments and correction to return to health. Step by step, healing is a process of stages. When the fulfillment of these steps and stages is made more important to you than the healing you desire, it's possible to increase your healing outcomes. To put it another way, when you make the journey of healing and the journey of releasing fear and embracing forgiveness more important than the goal of healing or the goal of managing fear and forgiveness, your chances of healing, releasing fear, and forgiving others and yourself increase tenfold.

Healing is possible when more of your energy is in the present moment. It's harder to heal if your energy is locked into the past or the future (remember the time portals chapter). You can't expect to heal when most of your energy is stuck in a painful past. By dwelling on the past, you hold your emotional energy and mental energy hostage there, so it isn't here now. It is also harder to heal if most of your energy is leaping forward into worrying or being afraid about the future. By letting your energy run ahead of you into the future, you hold your emotional and mental energy away from you, so it is also not here now. Herein lies the healing paradox mentioned earlier.

When you maintain a be-here-now approach to healing, where healing is a daily, hourly, or minute-by-minute process rather than a deadline sometime in the future, then your opportunities for healing unfold even more numerously and beautifully. You are relieved of the stress created by worrying or fear about the future, and you are relieved of the pressure that builds from constantly dwelling on the past. The past and future rob you of much-needed physical, emotional, mental energy in the present time. When your energy is present, your opportunities and outcomes for healing improve.

Sometimes the only person you need to forgive is you. You must forgive yourself for not forgiving yourself for your inability to forgive others. You can't expect to heal if you continue to berate yourself. Healing is a process. Bullying and berating yourself block that process. Instead of berating and bullying yourself, be kind to yourself. Instead of dwelling on the past or yearning for, or worrying about, the future, be here now. It is okay to be scared, but there is nothing to fear except fear itself and your fear of releasing that fear.

Notice what triggers fight, flight, freeze, or fawn for you—those trigger responses indicate waves of fear have crashed over you, and there is a need to come back to homeostasis. You can do this by breathing, bilateral tapping, and gently shaking your extremities. Once you are calmer, examine what triggered you and why; maybe revisit the portal on trigger wizardry to transmute the fear into something more useful. There is no shame in getting triggered or feeling fear take over; what is most important is that you intervene early to avoid living in fear or a toxic shame spiral.

Shame is the cancer of the psyche. It slowly eats away at us, tainting everything we experience with its dark glow of self-loathing. And it all stems from a lack of self-forgiveness and living in fear. Self-forgiveness is the practice of forgiving yourself for past wrongdoings. It involves changing your perception of yourself and what happened through the eyes of self-compassion and self-kindness and inner-standing. (See the atomic reframe portal for more on this healing and awakening tool.)

By inner-standing the deeper mechanics of why you did what you did and holding yourself in the embrace of self-love, you can let go, move on, and feel free again. It's necessary and unavoidable to have a certain level of guilt and/or shame after hurting ourselves or someone else (unless you're a sociopath and incapable of remorse, of course). Without guilt, we would sociopathically ignore the impact of our behavior. Can you imagine what society would be like if no one felt bad about what they had done? But guilt and shame become toxic when they begin to fester within us. Picture a stagnant pool of water—that's what a lack of self-forgiveness feels like.

There is no growth, no movement, no freshness, no life inside, only the same old, rancid sludge of self-hating thoughts and a fear of letting go.

In fact, when we carry toxic guilt and shame, we tend to create a negative and unrealistic image of ourselves in our minds. Such dark self-images sadly tend to create self-fulfilling prophecies or negative feedback loops. In other words, if we carry the negative core belief that we're cheating scumbags who don't have an ounce of loyalty within us, we may perpetuate that same behavior in our next relationship. If we carry the negative core belief that we're not good enough or are unworthy of love, then we may inadvertently or unconsciously sabotage all loving relationships or fear being loved deeply and authentically because we refuse to do so for ourselves first.

We must forgive ourselves for not forgiving ourselves for our inability to forgive others. We must stop being afraid of invisible boogie "menz"; and most importantly, we need to stop being afraid of ourselves and our inner power. Here's how self-forgiveness helps to resolve fear and so much more: We stop dwelling in and endlessly reliving the past. We begin living in the present. We have more hope for the future. We develop more self-love and inner-standing. We can more readily forgive others and release fears. We learn from our mistakes and transform as people. We have more energy and motivation for life. We learn how to become better people. Place one hand on your heart and the other on your forehead. Repeat these healing-vortex-within mantras:

> "I am willing to forgive my fears."
>
> "I choose to forgive myself and others more and more every day; I create more freedom for us all through the act of forgiveness."
>
> "I release the energy of fear on every level of my being by embracing the journey of forgiveness."

The Portal of Resistance

> What you resist, persists.
> —Carl Jung

Resistance and pain are inevitable parts of life, healing, and awakening. Remember the portal of paradox. Healing can be fun and easy, but sometimes it's just fucking hard, and we want to give up. We resist, and then we suffer. No judgment here. I've been there too, and I want to honor the resistance we all go through as we grow too (a little rhyme time helps the resistance). I'm sure many of you are still feeling some resistance to the previous chapter on fear and forgiveness. So I think a third F-WERD might be needed sometimes on this healing and awakening journey. Can you guess which F-WERD I'm thinking of? After a little F-bomb vocal release, we can all feel a little less resistant, ya dig. LOL.

We can all relate to that feeling of resisting getting out of bed in the morning to start the day, and what happens? The unpleasant thoughts, feelings, and sensations totally linger throughout that early part of the morning, sometimes all day. Remember the first healing vortex portal—being open to healing—and that other portal near Egypt about denial? Well, it's important that we also check for and honor uprisings of resistance that occur at any time on our journey through these portals of healing and awakening work. People can often become resistant to healing and awakening because they truly never end, and they can sometimes be incredibly challenging, especially if we're not practicing soul-*full* self-care on a regular basis. Resistance can be an incredibly healing and awakening experience. Resistance often shows us what our deepest fears are and areas in which we could use a little extra help.

Here are some potential portals of resistance that are normal part of the healing journey:

- Challenges asking for help or receiving assistance from anyone (trauma response)
- Addictions or challenging behaviors
- Compulsive distractions
- Procrastination
- Perfectionism
- Refusing to change unhelpful beliefs or thoughts
- Physical ailments (the body will manifest what the mind refuses to examine)
- Stuck in victim mentality ("poor me") or other low-vibe archetypes

Those who are simply engulfed in their emotional pain are often unwilling to be active participants in their healing journey on a conscious level. This is especially true if there are recent or raw issues around trauma or grief. Everyone heals in their own time, and it's important to be patient with ourselves in this given moment.

Too much time and energy have been spent rethinking, identifying, and honoring our wounds that we can be in danger of forgetting that the whole point is to get past these wounds and to get healthy. In fact, being healthy or succeeding at healing can scare some people, especially if there are deeply held beliefs that they don't deserve to be happy or healthy. Some people identify with their wounds, traumas, or pains and live their lives as proud victims, which is a sad way to live. We have also all been there at least once or twice.

The reason people don't heal or experience resistance is that they invest too much of their personal energy in past issues they refuse to release. For example, if a person holds a grudge against someone from their past, they must continually reinvest personal energy in that grudge daily and hourly. The energy that is going into a past event diverts valuable energy that could be here now, helping them heal. The person sends away the very healing energy that could be healing them. There is plenty of healing energy within each person to heal themselves, if only they weren't sending this energy out on unproductive missions.

When there is resistance, higher-self inquiry and intervention are required. What are you resistant to? Make a list of anything related to your healing journey that you experience resistance to or actively avoid. You might feel some resistance now to make this list; you can do it anyway, even just two or three bullet points. Come on, you know it will help you. Once you've made your resistance list, take three slow, long breaths and ask your higher self to take the wheel here. "Thank you, higher self, the best version of me, for giving me the strength to move through this resistance gracefully." Now, look over the list and notice that the things that trigger resistance are powerful portals to inner-standing and releasing fears, pain, trauma, and unaligned tomfoolery.

For additional support dissolving resistance and avoidance, repeat these healing-vortex-within mantras as often as needed:

> "Fuck resistance; I choose to move through resistance."
> "I choose to see any resistance I experience as insight into
> my fears and fuel for my healing and awakening journey.
> *Boom—alchemy bitch*!"
> "I am dissolving resistance and avoidance by letting my
> higher self take the wheel."

CHAPTER 32

The Portal of Meditations Fo Days

We tend to think of meditation in only one
way, but life itself is a meditation.
—Raul Julia

Most people don't like doing things they're not good at, including healing, inner work, and meditation. But you don't do inner work to be good at inner work. You don't meditate to become good at meditating. No one is grading you on how good you are—well, no one but yourself. And I highly encourage you to get the fuck out of that mindset *real* quick. I have heard many clients, friends, and family over the years say they aren't good at meditation. They don't enjoy the practice of it or have time to meditate. These are all bullshit excuses, and I know because I've used them all myself. The truth is that meditation is for everyone. There are so many ways to meditate, but finding the right one for you can be like searching for the perfect pair of shoes to wear when you meet RuPaul.

Most people think of transcendental meditation when they hear the word *meditation*, which refers to a silent practice used to tap into our natural ability to calm the mind down to achieve the least excited state of consciousness or "restful alertness and reflection." Transcendental meditation is a very popular type of meditation around the world, and it's the most scientifically studied. It has been shown to significantly decrease stress, depression, anxiety, and addiction issues; and improve countless physical ailments. Many people who use transcendental meditation regularly profess that it is better than sitting around and doing nothing. But let's keep it real. In this day and age of distractions and shorter and shorter attention spans, most of us have a hard time sitting still and focusing on our inner nothingness.

The good news is that there are dozens, if not hundreds, of different ways to meditate. Not all meditation styles are right for everyone. These practices require different skills and mindsets. How do you know which practice is right for you? Keep reading to learn more about the different types of meditation and how to get started. Although there isn't a right or wrong way to meditate, it's important to find a practice that meets your needs and complements your personality.

Mindfulness Meditation

Mindfulness meditation originates from Buddhist teachings and is the most popular meditation technique in the West. In mindfulness meditation, you pay attention to your thoughts as they pass through your mind—the "Teflon Mind," as we say in dialectical behavioral therapy (DBT). You don't judge the thoughts or become involved with them. You simply observe and take note of any patterns. This practice combines concentration with awareness. You may find it helpful to focus on an object or your breath while you observe any bodily sensations, thoughts, or feelings. This type of meditation is good for people who don't have a teacher to guide them, since it can be easily practiced alone.

Spiritual Meditation

Spiritual meditation is used in Eastern religions, such as Hinduism and Daoism, and in the Christian faith. It's like prayer, in that you reflect on the silence around you and seek a deeper connection with your God or universe. Essential oils are commonly used to heighten the spiritual experience. Popular options include frankincense, myrrh, sage, cedar, sandalwood, or Palo Santo (please be sure to buy from sustainable sources or plant and grow your own). Spiritual meditation can be practiced at home or in a place of worship. This practice is beneficial for those who thrive in silence and seek spiritual growth. Enjoying nature is also a spiritual *and* mindful meditation many people enjoy.

Focused Meditation

Focused meditation involves concentration using any of the five senses. For example, you can focus on something internal, like your breath, or you can bring in external influences to help focus your attention. Try counting mala beads, listening to a gong, or staring at a candle flame. This practice may be simple in theory, but it can be difficult for beginners to hold their focus for longer than a few minutes at first. If your mind wanders, it's important to come back to the practice and refocus.

Movement Meditation

Although most people think of yoga when they hear "movement meditation," this practice may include walking through the woods, gardening, practicing Qigong, and doing other gentle forms of motion. It's an active form of meditation where the movement guides you. Movement meditation is good for people who find peace in action and prefer to let their minds wander. This could also include dance meditation or any other type of movement that activates that mystical theta brainwave state we are so fond of in meditation practices. I find this style of meditation to be very grounding, especially when done in nature or while stretching in the sun.

Mantra Meditation or Chanting

Mantra meditation is prominent in many teachings, including Hindu and Buddhist traditions. This type of meditation uses a repetitive sound to clear the mind. It can be a word, phrase, or sound, such as "Ah" or "Om" or "*Badabing*." It doesn't matter if your mantra is spoken loudly or quietly. After chanting the mantra for some time, you will be more alert and in tune with your environment. This allows you to experience deeper levels of awareness. Some people enjoy mantra meditation because they find it easier to focus on a word than on their breath. This is also a good practice for people who don't like silence and enjoy repetition. You can choose any word or sound like *calm*, *relax*, or even *pickles*.

Guided Meditation or Guided Visualization

This style of meditation is particularly helpful for the visual person or if you are a visual learner. Commonly referred to as "guided meditation," "guided visualization," or "guided imagery meditation," this is a process in which someone meditates while focusing on an image, scene, or archetypal story. This imagery or scene allows a person to focus on different sensory aspects of the environment and moves through the imagery. This is one of my favorite types of meditation, and most of the meditations on my website include some form of guided imagery or visualization, including the "Meet Your Lemurian Dragon Meditation," in which you get to reconnect with your ancient dragon buddy.

Meditation Meditation—Meditate about Meditating

This is very silly, I know, but sometimes we need to meditate about meditating. How else are you going to figure out what styles of meditation work best for you? Give it a try, meditate about meditating, and see what comes up for you.

Body Scan or Progressive Muscle Relaxation (PMR)

This is a very helpful form of meditation that accomplishes two things: (1) helping the muscles of the body to release tension, which can directly reduce physical pain; and (2) helping us come back into the experience of sensations in our bodies, which can help the brain to send more pain-relieving signals. Most people either love or hate this one, but it is worth a try. It tends to work well before bedtime to ease the body into a more restful state for deep sleep.

Loving-Kindness Meditation

Also, referred to as "Metta" meditation, Loving-Kindness Meditation is an ultimate form of generous and selfless love toward ourselves and others. *Metta* is a Pali or Burmese word for benevolence, friendship, affection, and kindness. This form of meditation frees ourselves from any expectations or bindings and to activate the qualities of love, gratitude, compassion, and equanimity. It is also very helpful to use when working through challenging aspects of forgiveness of self and others.

Music or Sound Meditation

We all know how powerful sound is as well as music, healing frequencies or tones, or even just the sounds of nature. If you are more auditory, clairaudient, or just love sound baths, sound healing (and awakening), and gong extravaganzas, then this type of meditation might be the right fit for you. There are endless free music and sound meditations available on YouTube and various apps. Check out various offerings or apps and always do your research on the background of various sound frequencies to ensure they are a good fit for you.

Breathwork (or, as I like to call it, BreathWERK)

This is by far my favorite choice, and I will be covering this in its own very oxygenated chapter—right after this one. Breathwork meditation involves—you guessed it—*breathing*! We need to breathe to stay alive, but it is often the first thing we forget to do when stressed out, triggered, or in pain. Your breath is your most powerful tool; even just spending five minutes retraining your breathing per day so you are breathing slow, long, deep breaths from your diaphragm will completely transform your mind, body, and spirit. No apps or tools of any kind are needed for this one—just you and your breath.

Create Your Own Meditation

I cut back my workday on Mondays shortly after the 2020 pandemic dumpster fire crisis to enhance my self-care practices, spend more time with my soul, and write this (among many other) books. Mondays are lovingly referred to as Meditation Monday; Mental Health MacGyver Monday; or Mystical, Magical, and Mac Dre Monday—all of which were birthed from my weird brain because I couldn't find the exact kinds of meditations my soul yearned for, so I just started creating my own: Starseed Cosmic Consciousness, Lemurian Codes, Mental Health MacGyver Meditations, and the list goes on. This wonderfully creative "make your own meditation" led me to create and trademark my own unique style of breathwork—Starseed Cosmic BreathWERK®—and it is truly an intergalactic trip.

Mondays continue to be especially reserved for longer meditations (I love to meditate in some form every day), and the unique creations on which my brain and soul collaborated. I highly encourage you to create your own method of meditation now. Don't be afraid to step out of your comfort zone and try different types. It often takes a little trial and error until you find the one that fits. Meditation isn't meant to be a forced thing; if we're forcing it, then it becomes a chore. Gentle, regular practice eventually becomes sustaining, supportive, and enjoyable. Open yourself up to the possibilities. There are so many different forms of meditation that if one isn't working or isn't comfortable, just try creating a new one just for you. Use these healing-vortex-within mantras to further support your journey through the portal of meditation *Fo Days*:

> "I make time to regularly meditate in ways that help me go within."
> "Meditation is an act of self-love and soul-*full* self-care."
> "I choose to create my own ways to meditate and slow down."

CHAPTER 33

The Cosmic BreathWERK Portal

The trick to life is to just keep breathing.
—Johnny Lung, *The Respiratory Therapist*

Good ole Johnny Lung probably has the best damn quote in this whole book, ya dig. Johnny Lung is a pseudonym for this respiratory therapist dude, who has written many a good breath book and created a helpful website for other respiratory therapists. Good ole Johnny Lung has a very good point about the importance of breathing. Even though it seems obvious, most of us forget to breathe when we are stressed or triggered or just don't breathe correctly from our belly or diaphragm. A whole shit ton of unpleasant physical, mental, emotional, and energetic health problems can arise due to breathing improperly.

Be honest. Do you hold your breath when you're anxious or angry or triggered in some way? Do you breathe correctly in a slow, long, deep rhythm, making sure your stomach expands on the inhale every time? Most of us get caught in this very easy-to-solve breathing trick at some point or another. When we breathe in that shallow, upper chest way, we are getting less oxygen to our central nervous system. As a result, our entire bodies feel more tense, our brains don't work as well, and it's incredibly challenging to even hear the voice of our intuition.

When we slow down and breathe in this long and slow manner, checking to make sure our stomach expands on the inhale and lowers on the exhale, breathing in through the nose and out through the mouth, we become more centered, more oxygenated, and we feel better almost immediately. Try this now for three to five breaths—long, slow breaths, making sure the stomach expands. Do you feel better? Did you notice a shift of energy? I hope so. If not, keep practicing it until it works for you. Your breath is your most powerful tool for transformation, grounding, and coping with stress. Your breath can even get you high.

Did you know that the most naturally occurring amount of DMT is stored in your lungs? "WTF is DMT?" you might be asking. DMT or dimethyltryptamine is an essential amino acid tryptophan and precursor to serotonin (a.k.a. happy brain chemicals). It is a substance present in your brain when you are born and when you die, and the most naturally occurring amount of DMT between birth and death resides in the lungs. This is one reason why breathwork is so powerful and the scientific explanation for why you can "get high" on your breath or have deeply profound healing and awakening vision quests.

DMT is also an entheogen or consciousness-expanding psychoactive substance used and various cultures prepared for ritual purposes to connect with God, Spirit, or Source and our own divinity or soul. DMT is often referred as the "god molecule" or the "spirit molecule" because of this and the mystical, otherworldly experiences many people have who engage in breathwork and/or the use of plant medicines. You don't need to ingest anything, however, to feel the effects of DMT, which courses through your lungs every day. You just need to make time to breathe correctly and attend a breathwork session intermittently.

The lungs have more DMT receptors than anywhere else in the body. Through rhythmic breathing, you can access higher consciousness and journey on profound vision quests. Breathwork is a vehicle to rebirth yourself. This is one of the reasons I have found the portal of breathWERK to be the single most useful portal in the healing and awakening journey. Breathwork in general has changed my life, and it continues to assist me daily, not just in staying alive but in deeply living my life to the fullest. Breathwork allows us to tap into cosmic portals within ourselves and the greater universe. When your mind is frantically grasping onto what is real and what is false, you can feel the insanity set it. Return to the breath for a healing and awakening portal to freedom. Your breath will set you free, and you will finally see what is real and what is an illusion.

The most profound healing vortex journeys and the most intense shedding of past traumas have occurred for me time and time again during a breathwork session. I have had the pleasure of working with various styles of breathwork over the years including Sasha Cobra Tantric Breathwork, Transformational Breathwork, Rebirthing Breathwork, Holotropic Breathwork, and Neurodynamic Breathwork, which is a wonderful resource online for beginners to breathwork that I highly recommend.

Attending a breathwork session at least once a month is like doing a year of therapy in a few hours. I'm not exaggerating. Breathwork has truly saved my life and helped me to release trauma energy from my body in more powerful ways than any other healing modality. Breathwork has allowed me to restore my sense of safety within and to tap into greater spiritual sovereignty for myself and others. I love breathwork so much that I became certified in several modalities and even created my own. Starseed Cosmic BreathWERK is my unique creation in the BreathWERK portal. This is the one nearest and dearest to my heart and soul, Starseed Cosmic BreathWERK, which is essentially a starseed portal-guided visualization journey combined with transformational, galactic breathwork. It's out of this world … LOL.

Take a few moments now to tap back into your breath. Practice breathing slowly and deeply with long breaths in through the nose and out through the mouth. There's no need to pause or hold your breath. Just allow your breath to rhythmically flow in a slow, long manner in and out, making sure your stomach expands on the inhale. Take two to three minutes a day and retrain your breathing. You have two to three minutes for this; trust me, it will help you significantly. Over time, you will start to breathe deeper and feel more grounded; you will naturally breathe in this way, and this BreathWERK portal will always be available to you anywhere, anytime. You can also practice using these healing-vortex-within mantras to activate the BreathWERK portal:

> "My breath is the most powerful portal and tool I have to return to my center."
> "I am choosing to breathe long, slow, deep breaths every day."
> "Inhale the good shit, exhale the bullshit."

CHAPTER 34

The Portal to the Stars

From which stars have we fallen to meet each other here?
—Freidrich Nietzsche

Many indigenous cultures believed that some people incarnated here on Earth from the stars. In many Native American cultures, for example, people believe that souls enter the world through a hole in the sky. This hole is believed to be in the Pleiades star cluster. In mid-May, a natural cosmic phenomenon occurs, where this "hole in the sky" or the Pleiades star cluster appears to move behind the sun; this is called the "Pleiadian Alignment." When Earth, the sun, and the Pleiades are all in perfect alignment, they are in conjunction. The conjunct Pleiadian Alignment occurs in mid-May of every year, and an opposite alignment occurs with the Pleiades in mid-November. Earth, the sun, and the Pleiades are still in perfect alignment, but Earth is located between the sun and the Pleiades, creating a polarizing effect on the Pleiadian energy on Earth. It is believed that the energy of this natural, cosmic phenomenon that occurs twice a year helps starseed souls and others on Earth access powerful healing and awakening energies, integrate past and current life karmic lessons, and connect with the cosmic consciousness of higher dimensions.

Astrological alignments are also useful to connect with spirit guides or unlock soul gifts, memories, and dormant wisdom we all hold from past lives on Earth and elsewhere in this galaxy and beyond. When the sun and Earth are in line with a star system, it's easier to connect with a starseed spirit guide or cosmic ancestor from that star system. We all have spirit guides that are available to us when we need them, and yes, we may have more than one. They can be loved ones who have passed on, power animals, angels, starseed guides, or soul family. Our natal star charts can provide some insight into our most recent galactic origins or soul origins, but often we just feel a deep sense of knowing connected to certain constellations, planets, galaxies, or other dimensions. Trust your intuition on what you feel most connected to and use these methods in this portal chapter to connect more fully and regularly.

Please note that these are general recommendations. You can adjust these recommendations to best suit you and the starseed guides with whom you wish to connect. It is also important to note that you can connect to your cosmic guides or other spirit guides any day of the year. You don't need to wait for specific alignments to happen on the calendar. However, during specific alignments, the energies are more heightened, and you may find you can connect more fully or get more powerful messages and healing at those times. Many starseeds often report feeling very connected to specific ancient civilizations as well, such as ancient Egypt, ancient Sumeria, Lemuria, Atlantis, Alexandria, and Avalon—to name just a few.

The mainstream world of psychology and many other scientific disciplines regard astrology as a pseudoscience, claiming there is no empirical or evidence-based research supporting the validity or reliability of such information. I'm not trying to convince anyone here to think like I think about astrology, the stars, or aliens. I don't want you to think like me. I just want you to think. Thinking for myself and being a critical consumer of information are the only things that helped me *unfuck* my brain from the indoctrination of too many years of graduate school and traditional Western medicine.

The more I trusted my intuition and aligned with what made my soul happy, the more I kept gravitating back to astrology. The more I learned and researched about astrology, the more I realized how deeply intertwined it was with psychology and archetypes. In fact, I think of the twelve zodiac signs as twelve archetypes we can all embody and we all have in our star charts since each of the twelve zodiac archetypes rules each one of the twelve houses.

Carl Jung, triple OG psychiatrist, studied astrology and determined that the zodiac worked as a compendium of psychic realities. That is, he thought it made up "archetypes," which are more than a literary tool of psychoanalysis. Archetypes are psychological models or patterns that inhabit the collective unconscious. Jung's concept of synchronicity links psychoanalysis with astrology. Synchronicity refers to events that generate a coincidence. Jung and I agree that there is no such thing as a coincidence. According to Jung, everything from people, places, things, and life events is connected by invisible strings. Jung said, "Invisible forces exist that emanate from the universe. These forces are constantly intermixing and give rise to the events that happen in a person's life."

I have found time and time again the immense value in astrology and working with the stars for me and my clients. I'll never forget a very powerful double astrology chart reading I did for one of my clients and her husband. She sat there during the video call with her jaw dropped nearly the whole hour session as she proclaimed, "I had no idea it was this in depth and accurate. All this time I thought astrology was just about my birth date and sun sign. I am so glad you are teaching me how to use this now." I was thrilled to teach the many relevant layers to my client so she could better inner-stand why her and her husband communicated so differently despite having the same sun signs. They had very different Mercury placements (communication and thoughts) and very different Mars (action and passion) and Venus (love and relationships) placements—not to mention they had opposite Chiron (core wounds and hidden gifts) and North Node (karmic lessons and soul mission) placements. There is so much more than just our sun signs, people!

In fact, the more you learn about astrology, the more you realize how deep into space it goes as well as the power the stars and cosmic alignment portals possess to support your healing and awakening journey. Some of my most powerful insights and energy shifts have occurred when I revisit my natal and solar return charts (yes, you have a slightly varied chart every year too). Working with the magic of astrology, combined with meditating under the twinkling night stars and bathed in the golden rays of the sun during various cosmic alignments throughout the year, is my favorite thing to do, and I am truly grateful to share this magic with you and my soul clients.

Connecting to the vast galactic sea above and my starseed guides has only further anchored me into my soul mission and my purpose on Earth, and I highly recommend that you give it a try, even if you have no idea about starseeds, aliens, or astrology. Staring out into the vast night sky is a much needed reminder of how small our problems are in comparison to the eternal sky. You can do this any time of the year as well, not just during a specific alignment. Ironically, when we aren't in alignment with ourselves, the practice of tapping into the cosmic alignments above greatly re-centers us. Much like an astrological alignment, the mind, body, and spirit need consistent alignment as we navigate the healing vortex journey. What distractions do you need to turn away from more regularly (or permanently) to make getting aligned and staying aligned more efficient?

Cosmic alignments and stargazing are my bread and butter, baby, but if there is no inner alignment, our lives will also be chaotic. By working with the tools in this book, especially the mantras, you reach a state of homeostasis. You can find your inner alignment by nourishing the body and mind with the healing power of mantras and many of the other healing and awakening tools we have gone over to bring it all back into a state of balance. When you are balanced, you will know how to deal with the imbalance. Or you can also just go full supernova and explode all over the night sky in a gaseous, nebulous collapse. That would be some supercool star stuff too. The choice is yours. Believe in astrology or not, but please go stargazing immediately, if not sooner, and practice using these healing-vortex-within mantras:

> "I make time to get in alignment with the stars and sun,
> and within my life."
> "I am a supernova with a soul."
> "I choose to see the stars in the night sky as a reminder to
> honor both the darkness and the light within me."

CHAPTER 35

The Portal of the Atomic Reframe

> The talk of atomic energy in terms of atomic bombs is like
> talking of electricity in terms of the electric chair.
> —Pyotr Kapitsa

When most people hear "atomic energy," they think of the atomic bomb, war, and the horrific devastation caused by the use and abuse of this powerful source of energy. But when we think about both the scientific and spiritual inner-standing of atomic energy, it becomes a powerful portal along our healing and awakening journey. Atomic energy is the source of nuclear power. In nuclear physics and nuclear chemistry, a nuclear reaction is a process in which two nuclei, or a nucleus and an external subatomic particle, collide to produce one or more *new* nuclides. Thus, a nuclear reaction must cause a *transformation* of at least one nuclide to another. I don't know about you, but I have a major physics boner right now.

Atomic energy is also the source of the explosive force of an atomic bomb. The first nuclear explosion on Earth took place on July 16, 1945, when a plutonium implosion device was tested in New Mexico. Hoisted atop a one-hundred-foot tower, this plutonium device released 18.6 kilotons of power, instantly vaporizing the tower and turning the surrounding asphalt and sand into green glass. Exactly seventy-five years later, on July 16, 2020, an atomic bomb exploded in my life—metaphorically speaking—when I survived a near-death experience that drastically changed the internal and external landscape of my life forever.

I could have stayed stuck in a victim mentality and spiraled into never-ending despair, but after surviving, I chose to see that experience as a blessing in disguise that had to happen to put me on a better timeline and further activate my soul mission. The blast of that atomic trauma destroyed what needed to be released so I could become a better version of myself. I am still dealing with the fallout of the blast, and the gory details of what happened are less important than the message here: reframing the bombs that explode and implode in our lives is tapping into the atomic energy of our perception, transmutation, and transformation abilities. Practicing the *atomic reframe* is deeply cathartic. If I can do it after the worst trauma of my life, so can you. You can reframe anything. *Anything.*

What is a reframe? A reframe is a technique psychologists, therapists, coaches, and healers of all kinds often use to create a different way of looking at a situation, person, relationship, or experience. It is one of the most helpful healing and awakening tools I have used over and over again both personally and professionally.

We all have thought patterns that are overly negative and unrealistic at times. These are called "cognitive distortions," and they include polarized thinking or all-or-nothing thinking, catastrophizing, overgeneralizing, discounting the positive, personalizing, labeling, emotional reasoning, mind reading, and making should statements—or, as I like to call it, "should-ing on yourself." These are chronic errors in thinking, and they often cause unnecessary distress and suffering. A reframe helps us to see the shades of gray, alternative explanations, objective evidence, and positive or neutral interpretations to expand our thinking, consciousness, and energy.

What is an atomic reframe? An atomic reframe takes the basic bitch reframe to a new level—it's an *extreme* reframe with a more powerful ripple effect or blast, if you will. An atomic reframe is needed to change our perception of the worst traumas and biggest blazing dumpster fires in life. In my work with trauma survivors for nearly two decades, I often use the atomic reframe technique to guide clients to see the atomic bombs of trauma and horrific experiences as portals for learning, resiliency, and activation of their inner post-traumatic growth. This can take time to move through the portal of feelings and various other necessary healing and awakening portals before we are ready to detonate the atomic reframe portal. It is one of the most beautiful and inspiring parts of the work I do to bear witness to a client when they atomically reframe a terrible childhood trauma, abusive partner, or the death of a loved one. The activation of this portal signifies pivotal progress on the healing and awakening journey.

When we change our perception of events, situations, traumas, people, and anything else that is out of our control, we take our power back and inspire others to do the same.

Perception is everything. The sinking of the *Titanic* was a miracle to the lobsters on that ship. To change ourselves effectively and sustainably, we need to change how we look at everything; we need to change our perception. We all know we have very little control in life, even though most of us don't like to confront that hard truth. The good news is that we do have control over our perception and how we choose to activate the atomic reframe portal on our healing and awakening journey. We have all experienced a metaphorical bomb dropping on our lives at least once— especially after surviving the year 2020. We will all experience at least one, if not *many*, heartbreaks or traumas along our journey in life. A heartbreak isn't always as loud as a bomb exploding. Sometimes it could be as quiet as a feather falling and the most painful thing is, nobody hears it but you.

I often think about how a caterpillar turns to mush during its process of becoming a butterfly. Or how I love the Japanese tradition of Kintsugi, which involves mending cracked pottery with gold to create something even more beautiful because of having been broken and restored.

Try reframing a mildly distressing situation, relationship, or experience now. You might find it helpful to write down your original thought, followed by any cognitive distortions or unhelpful thinking patterns. Next, write down three or four alternative interpretations to your original thought. Then perform a cost-benefit analysis by analyzing how your thought patterns have helped you cope in the past. Do they give you a sense of control where you feel powerless? Do they allow you to avoid taking responsibility or healthy risks? Ask yourself what holding on to that initial cognitive distortion costs you. Weighing the pros and cons of your thought patterns motivates you to change them, reframe them, and take your power back.

If you found this helpful, repeat the above process with an atomic situation in your life or the world. This time choose something that moderately to severely distresses you or has been holding you back on your healing and awakening journey. How can you atomically reframe this? How will the nuclear ripple effect of this atomic reframe help you and others?

Enhance this atomic reframe process before and after it with the power of the sound of your voice. Place one hand on your heart and the other on your forehead and repeat these healing vortex mantras loudly and proudly—like-a-bomb loud. Just don't wake up your neighbors.

> "I choose not to allow disasters and mistakes to define my day or my life."
> "I have survived many tough situations, and I will survive now."
> "I choose to atomically reframe the dumpster fire train wrecks in life that are out of my control and take my power back."

CHAPTER 36

Portals to Hell and Other Cautionary Tales

It's a lot easier to fool someone than to
convince them they've been fooled.
—Unknown

I heavily debated whether to include this chapter in the book, since I have already taken us through the protection and OPP portal chapters, but this is a topic that has tremendous healing and awakening power to share, so here I am talking about "Portals to Hell and Other Cautionary Tales." Please know that I share this information with you not to scare you but to provide some useful personal and professional experience on potential traps and mirages along the way to the healing and awakening vortex oasis within. Take what resonates and leave what doesn't.

Have you ever seen or experienced a portal to hell? (Insert creepy Halloween music here.) One such incident sticks out in my mind in which I experienced a physical portal to hell in this dude's apartment in one of those old, turn-of-the-century buildings in Hayes Valley in San Francisco. It was the most intense experience. I literally sensed the portal in the corner of the living room of this guy's apartment that I had been dating for a couple of months. He thought I was crazy, but I assured him I didn't suffer from insanity. I enjoyed every minute of it.

Seriously, these nefarious portals are lurking all around us, and we all know San Francisco has a history of paranormal activity fo' sho. The longer I hung out in the dude's apartment, the sicker I became. After less than an hour, I became violently ill and had to step outside for fresh air.

I immediately felt better and ended our hangout early to drive home. By the time I got home, I felt totally fine again and knew something was way off about this guy and his portal to hell of a home.

While there are physical locations that have a hellish or unaligned vibe with us, most of the portals to hell I refer to aren't quite so obvious or visible. Let us begin by exploring some of these other "portals to hell" so you can stay grounded and aligned on your inner journey and avoid the inferno of the underworld that opposes true healing and awakening.

What is toxic positivity? Toxic positivity is like the dark side of optimism. "Good vibes only." "Look on the bright side." "Only focus on the positive." Though these are well-intentioned phrases, engaging in toxic positivity results in the denial, minimization, and invalidation of the authentic human emotional experience. By disallowing the existence of certain feelings, we end up with repressed emotions, guilt, shame, and a fundamental rejection of wholeness and integration. Remember the portal less traveled on Shadow WERK? I know brushing off things that bother us or hiding our true feelings is an unhealthy coping habit we have all engaged in at some point, but for some this has gotten much worse in recent years.

If anything, the pandemic has exacerbated the problem with toxic positivity and the denial of the depth of the tyranny happening all around us. The global pandemic is a clear example of where repressed emotions can be harmful to a person's health. Since this has been a far-reaching event that has affected everyone on the planet, there have also been varying degrees of suffering. Messages of hope and optimism have a different effect from those of positivity because they also acknowledge the negative. Whereas if we are being told to focus only on the good or on all the ways we are better off than others, we will never get the chance to confront our very real pain. No, things are not "going back to normal," and they never were normal to begin with. We are just more aware of that fact now. In confronting the hard realities in life, we can more appropriately deal with them, and we don't get sucked into a portal to hell without even knowing.

Spiritual bypassing is another example of a portal to hell. What is spiritual bypassing? Spiritual bypassing describes a tendency to use spiritual explanations to avoid complex psychological issues. It is a way to hide behind spirituality or spiritual practices to avoid facing unresolved emotional issues, psychological wounds, or a variety of other hardships in life. It is a combination of spiritual delusion and healing and awakening avoidance. It prevents people from acknowledging what they are feeling and distances them from both themselves and others, effectively sucking people farther and farther away from their healing vortex within and into an unhelpful portal or portal to hell. Some examples of spiritual bypassing include the following:

- avoiding feelings of anger
- believing you are superior to others because of your spirituality
- using spirituality to avoid difficult emotions
- believing that all spiritual practices are always positive
- extremely high, and often unattainable idealism
- focusing only on spirituality and not on the present or practical
- projecting negative feelings onto others
- chronically using defense mechanisms of denial and repression

Being aware of spiritual bypassing helps us ensure we don't fall into this trap.

One of the most dangerous and devious portals to hell is spiritual materialism. What is spiritual materialism? Let's be real for a moment and admit that sometimes our healing and awakening practices can harm us more than help us. When our spiritual practices reinforce, bolster, and underhandedly inflate our sense of self (the ego), this is spiritual materialism. It is a form of toxic spirituality and a portal to hell, as I call it. In this capitalist-driven society, it is so freakin' easy to fall into spiritual materialism and not even realize it (or be in denial about it). Examples of spiritual materialism include the following:

- Owning and indirectly claiming a special status due to certain gifts (we are not better than or separate from others because we communicate with spirits, read auras, or have extrasensory gifts)
- Buying into the spiritual marketplace and chasing after endless workshops, methods, tools, and trinkets, which promise to make you wiser or more spiritual (the intention is so important when we purchase anything and to check the ego to see whether compulsive buying becomes an issue)

- Using any spiritual practice to attract or manifest your desires because it would "make you happier" rather than being grateful for what you already have
- Becoming addicted to self-improvement (this one hits home for me as a healer, and we have to check it when it comes up and revisit the reality check portal if needed)
- And the list goes on and on

We have all been there, and there is no shame in admitting or recognizing any of this behavior in yourself now. To stay aware moving forward of these spiritual traps or portals to hell, ask yourself periodically, *how is this belief, practice, or tool reinforcing the ego or the separate sense of self?*

Finally, we come to the last section on portals to hell and other cautionary tales on the healing and awakening vortex within the journey. People in the spiritual community talk a lot about false light but not enough about false darkness. What is false light? What is true light? What is false darkness? What is true darkness? I'm glad you asked. Remember: the goal is to be whole and integrate rather than polarize. There are true light and true darkness in our world. There are false light and false darkness in our world. The key to discovering true light and true darkness is in the realization that all true light opposes false darkness and all true darkness opposes false light. True light and true darkness are not in opposition to one another. They exist as compliments to one another, just as false darkness compliments false light. Without this inner-standing, one can easily mistake true darkness for false darkness or false light for true light. You might be thinking, *WTF is this lady talking about—it's all light, so what's the difference?* Let me elaborate.

True light is the light of love. It is opposed by false darkness, which is fear. True darkness is the womb or matrix out of which all reality comes into being. False light is make-believe. Make-believe isn't imagination. Imagination is an image held with true intent, whether it becomes reality or not. Make-believe is deception; it is an image of reality passed along to others, with no real intention of creating the reality that is mocked up. False light is deception. True light (love) comes forth from true darkness (the womb), and false light (deception) creates false darkness (fear). Source, prime creator, or God (service to the collective or others) is the author of the true light that springs forth from the matrix of reality. This simple principle allows us to better inner-stand why our world is so full of darkness. Portals to hell (Satan, Lucifer, or service-to-self douche-lord factions) deceive the whole world. A portal to hell or service-to-self entity creates and spreads false light toward the creation of false darkness. Obviously, so much more could be said about this portal to hell and the subject of light versus darkness, especially false light versus false darkness. For now, observe the world in which we live in light of this invaluable truth and see what emerges. Always trust your intuition and go within for true resonance with all things, beings, and information.

Furthermore, I want to share that I have personally gotten caught up in all these portals to hell more than once, so please don't be hard on yourself if you realize you might have visited or are currently stuck in one yourself. There is always a way out of the depths of hell once you realize that is where you might be stuck. The importance of discernment, dedication, and accountability along your healing and awakening journey is of the utmost importance. The shadow side of spirituality is real and alive despite what many would like to believe. The reality is that if we're not mindful and discerning, we can easily fall into the traps of spiritual bypassing (or using spirituality to avoid reality), spiritual narcissism, spiritual codependency, cult mentality, spiritual pride and ego traps, and false light and false darkness portals to hell.

If you find this portal particularly confronting, don't worry. Most people do. After all, for many people, spirituality is the only place that feels safe and like home. Not only that, but we tend to solely associate spirituality with love and light; this is often referred to as "toxic positivity." It will serve you well to honor both the hard and uplifting elements on your healing and awakening journey and throughout all aspects of life, love, death, and beyond. This is important to inner-stand and face with honesty and courage.

It ain't all love and light, but that stuff is wonderful and needed. Keep things in balance and honor when you need to cry or be angry in healthy ways. Don't bypass the hard stuff just to be blissed out all the time. That's really no different from using drugs, alcohol, TV, food, love, or sex to distract from the real work. If you know you are prone to addictive behavior, move forward on your healing journey, being very mindful that you balance the hard work with play—the shadow with the light WERK. Too much of anything can create other issues. And please reach out for support to a trained professional if you need more support in overcoming an addiction.

Practice using these healing-vortex-within mantras for further discernment around portals to hell and other cautionary tales:

> "I am consciously creating balance and discernment in all areas of my life."
> "I choose to align with a balance of true light and true darkness, and I transcend polarization within and around me."
> "I am informed and aware of potential portals to hell, and I protect myself and my energy."

The Hilarious Portal: Laughter Is a Sacred Vortex

I would say laughter is the best medicine, but it's more than
that. It's an entire regimen of antibiotics and steroids.
—Steven Colbert

The only things I prescribe to my clients—and the world—are deep thoughts, authenticity, self-care, and of course, laughter. Laughter is medicine, and it won't make you unable to reach orgasm, like so many pharmaceuticals heavily prescribed to treat mental health challenges like depression, anxiety, and trauma. However, crippling mental, emotional, physical, and spiritual health issues aren't always so hilarious. If you've ever struggled with chronic, debilitating, soul-crushing health concerns, like depression or trauma, then you know exactly how hard it can be to get out of bed, let alone smile or laugh or find joy in anything.

The old saying "Laughter is the best medicine" has a lot of truth to it. Laughter has tons of healing properties that aren't just limited to healing and awakening or mental health concerns. Laughter has numerous positive physical effects, from promoting longevity to boosting the immune system. Laughter is like jogging for your mind, heart, and soul because a good ole belly laugh gives every system of the body a workout. Laughter perks up your heart, increases circulation, lowers blood pressure, boosts your lungs and diaphragm muscles, and breaks up tension in the face. The vibrating muscles of a big laugh also give you an internal massage. See, laughter is like a trainer, coach, and masseuse all in one. The best part is it doesn't cost you a dime!

Laughter also helps people to get over chronic illness but most importantly the fear and anxiety about the illness, which can set up a stressful cycle of pain and fear. That worsens the prognosis. Humor can break the chronic ailments by releasing endorphins, the body's natural painkillers. I mean IBS, migraines, crippling PTSD, and a dislocated elbow named Flexy Leverson—fucking hilarious! How do I know? Because I've suffered from them all (and more fun conditions), and I've also healed them or kept them more manageable with a balance of trill healing WERK and laughter. While we don't want to use humor to bypass real healing (remember the portals-to-hell chapter), we can use humor and laughter to enhance and expedite our healing and awakening journey. If it's not fun and funny sometimes, what's the point?

Did you know that laughter can also heal the brain? I mentioned before that I laugh a lot with my clients during individual therapy, coaching, and healing sessions. Sure, we work through difficult emotions too, but I know that if my clients are suffering from grief or depression, laughing at a funny joke can bring momentary relief. This can be profoundly healing for a depressed person with low or suppressed pleasure-enhancing chemicals in the brain. Since depression also suppresses the immune system, having a good laugh can decrease stress hormones like epinephrine and cortisol. Laughter reverses the suppression of serotonin and dopamine by triggering the release of feel-good neurochemicals such as endorphins and activates the pleasure pathways in the brain. Laughter "braingasms" anyone?

Physiologically, laughter is the exact opposite of the stress response. Stress and tension elevate stress and hormones, tighten muscles, constrict blood vessels, upset the brain's neurochemistry, depress the immune system, and overload the heart. Laughter relieves tension, lowers stress hormones, improves the brain's neurochemistry, settles the heart, and boosts the immune system. So travel down the Hilarious Portal *daily*; it's good for your health. Prescribe yourself a daily laughter challenge for seven days. See if you feel any better. Here are seven one-liner puns to get you started. A pun a day keeps the doctor away, ya dig:

1. Geology ROCKS! But Geography is where it's AT!
2. If attacked by a mob of clowns, go for the juggler.
3. The rotation of Earth really makes my day.

4. Pollen is what happens when flowers can't keep it in their plants.
5. Will glass coffins be a success? Remains to be seen.
6. Most people are shocked when they find out how bad an electrician I am.
7. Never trust atoms; they make up everything.

Commit to a daily or weekly laughter ritual, practice, and/or routine. Get in touch with your unique sense of humor. Dad jokes are not for everyone, but my inner old man and my inner child just fucking loves them. It's important that you tap into your unique sense of humor, though. What makes you laugh? How can you make more time in your day-to-day routine to laugh, smile at life's absurdity, or even just be silly? Remember: laughter is a high vibrational state of energy, and you will feel better if you honor the power it has to heal and uplift us all. Life is too serious to be taken seriously all the time. Use these healing-vortex-within mantras as well:

> "I choose to make time every day to smile and laugh."
> "I honor and activate my unique sense of humor."
> "I am a laugh factory that raises the vibration of my healing vortex within."

CHAPTER 38

The Portal of Love

Love is not a relationship with someone. Love is a way of life.
—Unknown

What is love? It's not just a catchy '90s dance song from *A Night at the Roxbury*. Love is no doubt a ginormous and nebulous topic of infinitude. I simply had to include it in the healing and awakening portals because to me, love truly *is* a way of life. I have learned this time and time again. All stories are love stories. And this next story I'm going to share with you is about the love of my life, Disco Tom Cat. An entire library of glorious books could be written about the one, the only Disco Tom Cat Hobson. And if I live long enough, an entire library of cat books *will be*. Meow.

Disco Tom was a one-of-a-kind *man cat*. Disco Tom Cat was a bunny rabbit, bear man, lion-tiger Lyran starseed hybrid soul, first of his name and rightful heir to the Iron Cat Tree Throne. He was also a cat if you want to be basic about it. Disco Tom was almost a wiener dog. That's right. I had wanted a pet of my own for some time, and I put a deposit down for a dachshund wiener dog puppy of a new litter a friend was breeding. Sadly, the wiener pups were not well and perished just after they were born. I thought my dreams of finally having my own pet were kaput. I surrendered the matter to the care of the universe, and the next day I got a call from another, crazier friend, who was getting evicted from her apartment and had a litter of baby kittens just barely six weeks old.

"I'll take one fo sho!" I told her with delight.

She described what each one looked like. "There's an all-black one, a calico one, two white ones, a white-and-gray one—"

I interrupted her and knew immediately. "That one! The gray and white one!"

Two hours later, I drove to her house to pick up Tom. I knew I was going to name him Tom from the jump because he looked like the gray-and-white cat from the Tom and Jerry cartoons. The disco came a few months later when I discovered he loved disco music. I had literally nothing prepared to have a baby kitten. No food, no litter box, no cat carrier. So I just tucked baby Tom in between my boobs, zipped up my jacket, and drove to the store with him to buy everything we needed.

During the first year of his life, Tom very rarely left my side. I took him everywhere with me. He gave me so much love and a purpose and such a grounding force in my life during a time when I was completely lost. Disco Tom loved everyone, and everyone loved Disco Tom. He made a lasting impression on everyone he crossed paths with, especially the one shady neighbor he didn't like in Humboldt, whose head he jumped on once to defend me. What a good boy!

My friend gifted me with this fabulous book called *Careers for Your Cat*, and it had a "MEOWERS-BRIGGS" personality test to fill out on behalf of your cat to discover the career that best suited their personality. Disco Tom's ideal career was "TV News Anchorman," and I cannot even begin to tell you how well this suited him, right down to his little collection of bowties he loved to wear.

I'll never forget this one New Year's Eve when Disco Tom Cat was about eight years old, and my mom had gifted him with a dapper, red bowtie. We put it on him and went out that night to a show, and when we came home many hours later, Tommy was not only still wearing the red bowtie; he was posing like a Burt Reynolds *Playgirl* poster centerfold in all his charm and regal handsomeness. I told my group of friends, "I think he likes to dress up." And from there the outfits kept getting gifted and collected, and he sure did love to dress up; it was weird and unique for a cat to be so into it, but who am I to deny a male supermodel cat his photo shoot fantasy, right? Disco Tom Cat was the most interesting and beloved man cat in the world … nay … in the universe … no, no … in the multiverse … in all past, present, and future timelines, across all dimensions of time and space beyond eternity and back to the galactic core of *all*. It's Disco Tom Cat. Oh, yes … it has always been Disco Tom Cat.

Disco Tom Cat wasn't just the love of my life; he taught me how to truly love myself and others. Shit, he even helped me write my dissertation. He was such a sweet man cat, and he stuck by my side through nearly sixteen years of craziness and school and boyfriends and girlfriends. Oh my! He was the one constant *love* in my life, and I truly didn't think I would survive when he passed away.

Tommy had been battling kidney failure for a few years, and I began working with a wonderful vet, Dr. Sarah Daniels, who did house visits to minimize stress on sick animals. I knew I didn't have control over how long he lived or when he decided to cross over, but I did ask Tom and the most high God to please just let me be there with him when he went. You see, I never got a proper goodbye with any other pet I had lost as a child or any of my close family or friends or clients who had died over the years. Grief is a lot harder for most of us to process and cope with if we don't get to say goodbye or see the dead body. All mammals are this way.

As hard as it was to say goodbye to my firstborn fur baby, I am forever grateful that he died peacefully at home in my arms. I am so incredibly grateful to everyone who supported me during this time and the love I was able to find within myself to get me through one of the hardest losses of my life. Grief is just love wearing a scary Halloween mask disguise. Disco Tom gave me so much love for nearly sixteen years, and that love is always with me. I even started a tradition on his birthday every year when I dress up like him to keep his spirit and *the love* within alive. Cats never die; they just fall asleep in your heart. RIP, Disco Tom Cat. January 31, 2004–October 2, 2019.

Loving yourself has very little to do with self-help book gurus telling you to stand in front of the mirror and have some cathartic tearful moment, in which you meditate away decades of self-hatred. There was nothing, literally nothing, I thought would help me survive the loss of Disco Tom. No bubble bath helped. No amount of crying or pizza made the pain go away. The only thing I realized would help me survive was love. Love for myself and honoring the love I had shared with my fur baby. Love is sometimes the hardest choice though.

What is self-love? Put simply, self-love is the practice of inner-standing, embracing, and showing compassion for yourself. Self-love involves nurturing your entire being—that means taking care of yourself on physical, emotional, mental, and spiritual levels. When engaging in self-love, we also work to forgive ourselves, accept our flaws, and embrace our inner demons. Loving yourself means you're not a doormat, have respect for yourself, and ensure you are treated in ways that don't demean you. You don't allow yourself to play a victim role, and you reclaim your power through accountability. Loving yourself means you are kind to yourself in all ways. This means you aren't verbally abusive to yourself in your thoughts. You also remember to take care of your physical needs through rest, exercise, and healthy eating. Loving yourself means you accept that you will never be perfect and forgive yourself for mistakes. Loving yourself is accepting that you are strong and worthy, even during your darkest hour.

The truth is, all these portals are portals of love. Every story is a love story. Everything and everyone in the entire cosmos are connected by the unifying thread of love, ya dig. I know you love something, no matter how small it may be, about yourself and/or your life. Focus on that one small thing and build up from there. You are loved. *You are love.* Please know that I am always holding a space of love for you, no matter how shitty you may feel. Repeat these healing-vortex-within mantras (and create your own too for increased self-love and self-healing):

> "I choose to love myself in practical, useful ways each day."
> "I define what loving myself means to me."
> "I am learning to navigate the self-love journey; I am learning to love and accept myself."

CHAPTER 39

The Portal of SoulWERK, Soulgasms, and Soul Boners

The most powerful weapon on earth is the human soul on fire.
—Ferdinand Foch

What is a soul? It's like electricity—we don't really know
what it is, but it's a force that can light a room.
—Ray Charles

We have covered many of the WERKS of healing and awakening thus far, including shadow, light, and electric inner child (WERK, that is). Now we get to the advanced WERKS—SoulWERK. SoulWERK is the process of bringing the essential self—the soul—out of hiding. It's a fundamental shift away from occupying the constructed self and toward the art of living from our souls. SoulWERK begins with the knowledge that the soul is always trying to move us toward wholeness. SoulWERK is the path of reuniting you with your eternal essence again. When you learn how to listen to and reclaim your eternal essence, or soul, you experience what awakened beings through the ages refer to as nirvana or enlightenment. It is the ability to transcend suffering, embody unconditional love and peace, and live authentically again. Furthermore, when we live from the soul, we are immediately able to inner-stand our sacred life purpose.

However, SoulWERK requires real dedication and commitment. To discover the truth of who we are, we must set out on the path of the lone wolf or spiritual seeker. While others can support and nourish this path, it is ultimately a solitary path that demands courage, persistence, and the willingness to dig deep.

The purpose of SoulWERK is to help us mature on all levels and dimensions as spiritual beings having a human experience. As we make our way through the winding and often perilous paths of our inner underworlds, we reclaim the soul gifts of empathy, sensitivity, self-responsibility, strength, truth, and inner harmony. SoulWERK is a life's work, and when you allow your soul to WERK in the way that ignites your passion, you experience what I call "soul boners and soulgasms." Soul boners and soulgasms are hilarious metaphors for that state of spiritual bliss. The *Urban Dictionary* defines a *soulgasm* as "a moment of pure spiritual ecstasy, in which, an artful piece of life touches and moves the very core of your being, forcing you to closes your eyes, gasp slightly and lose yourself in its beauty, and as you do, a delightful tingling sensation flourishes from the back of your head and travels down your neck to ravish the entirety of your flesh." Sounds delightful! And this is a lovely outcome of SoulWERK, other healing vortices within portal adventures, and acts of service and doing good things for others and the world at large as we will see in the next section on soul boners.

The *Urban Dictionary* defines a soul boner as "the technical description for what's otherwise known as 'warm and fuzzy' or 'spiritually lascivious'; generally, a 'deep down inside' kind of feeling that expresses delight and gratification." Basically, it's a boner that both men and women of *all* ages can acquire at any moment in time. Soul boners can be caused by a large portion of the emotional spectrum, spanning from excitement to amazement to downright badass-ness. Take a few moments and think about what causes soul boners and soulgasms for your soul. Why do these things give you a soul boner or soulgasm? This is an important question since it can help you better inner-stand and over-stand your soul purpose or soul mission here on earth. Keep a running list and add to it when you experience a moment of soul bliss. To further activate your soul WERK portal, use these healing-vortex-within mantras:

> "I honor my soul by doing the things that light me up deeply from within."
> "I am WERKing my soul daily by cultivating a loving relationship with myself."
> "I give myself permission to experience soulgasms and soul boners on the regular; I do what makes my soul ecstatic."

CHAPTER 40

Unlocking the Portal to Your Unique Self-Healing Superpowers

All the quirks you've spent years trying to hide, they are
actually your superpowers; they're what set you apart.
They don't make you better. They don't make you worse.
They make you *you*, and only you can be that.
—Oliver Stark

Everyone has a unique self-healing superpower. It is true. The trick is figuring out how to unlock the code to this unique self-healing superpower portal so you may travel even further into the healing vortex within and achieve multidimensional self-mastery. You can rapidly repair your mind, body, and spirit in such a magical way that you begin to level up in ways you never thought possible. Think about how our bodies heal when we get a cold or break a bone. A good healing outcome depends on your mental attitude. You can rapidly regenerate, not just cellular tissues but also DNA. You have everything you need within you right now for accelerated healing, spiritual downloads, transmuting stagnant symptoms, shifting limiting beliefs, and destroying the negative energy that has been holding you back.

Often, the exact thing we have felt makes us "broken" or wounded or flawed in some way *is* actually a self-healing superpower when we activate the atomic reframe portal. How many of us empaths and starseeds have been told we are too sensitive. I know I heard this a whole shit ton growing up and well into my adulthood. I even thought it was a curse to be so hyperaware and deeply affected by the people, places, and things around me. But then I started applying the lessons I've learned and traveling more and more through my inner portals, and I was able to fully activate and own my self-healing superpowers. Sensitivity *is* a superpower! Maybe you have been told you are "too bossy" or "daydream too much" or are "too soft-spoken." Maybe those aren't the fatal flaws you once thought they were but instead can be atomically reframed into "a leader who can start their own business" or "a creative visionary" or "a gentle soul who works well with children and animals." It's all about perspective, as you can see.

Take some time now and write down a few traits or behaviors you feel insecure about or have been told are bad. Next, place both hands on your heart as you breathe slowly and deeply and connect to your soul. Do this for four to five minutes and then come back to your list. How can you apply the atomic reframe, soul WERK, and countless other portals you have traveled through to see this trait or behavior as a superpower? Do this regularly to unlock your self-healing superpowers. Allow yourself to be creative in how you look at your superpower abilities.

For even further support in unlocking the codes to your self-healing superpowers, you can deep-dive into your star chart, solely focusing on these two aspects: Chiron and the North Node. These are two highly underrated and often missed aspects in our natal star charts. Chiron relates to our core wound, *but* (and it's a big ole Centaur *butt*) it also shows us our self-healing superpowers. Chiron in Greek mythology was a healer who couldn't heal himself. In our natal star charts, the placement and house in which Chiron resides reveal to us insight into our core wound. Not only is Chiron a wonderful portal of healing; it is also a cosmic key to unlocking your soul's gifts and self-healing superpowers. The Chiron glyph symbol even looks like a key. You can look yours up online along with the North Node for some powerful insights and activations.

The North Node relates to important life lessons and our souls' purpose or soul mission. Think about how many of us struggle to get to the core of healing and find our purpose in life. Yet just as plain as day in our astrology charts, these insights provide powerful activation codes for inner- and over-standing ourselves, the root of our healing and awakening mission, and our soul mission. Wowie, wow, wowza. It's worth taking a peek at your placements, even if you think astrology is baloney.

I highly encourage you to say the self-healing superpower portal mantras while doing a power pose (in other words, a body position that will help you activate your personal power and channel guidance to your self-healing superpowers). Stand up straight, feet firmly planted on the ground (preferably barefoot in the Earth), and place both hands on your hips or any other power pose and say these healing vortex mantras loudly and proudly as many times as needed to unlock your self-healing superpowers now:

> "I have regenerative self-healing superpowers."
> "Wounds are the keys to unlocking my self-healing superpowers, and I transmute pain to into power."
> "I am activating my self-healing superpowers now."

CHAPTER 41

The Portal of Vision Hunting

When you know your WHY, you'll know your WAY.
—Michael Hyatt

Vision hunting is a term used to describe the quest for your "ultimate why." Your ultimate is the why behind everything you do. When you find your ultimate why, you'll know your ultimate way—in this life and beyond. My ultimate why is truly the core message of this book—that we all have the ability to heal and awaken ourselves. My why, I have also discovered, is love—like true Lemurian-Pleiadian Starseed, I have dedicated my life to reminding others of their innate self-healing superpowers, to learn that love isn't a relationship with someone but a way to be with all things. Love is a frequency that is one of the highest vibrations of energy we can activate. Knowing this has paved a clear path in my life, and it daily guides me both personally and professionally. But it took me over thirty-five years to find my why and my way of sorts; my why and my way are also ever evolving and flexible, so I can continue to grow and fine-tune as needed. We know the work is never really done, and this is what makes the journey more interesting and fun when we allow it to be. There is no set destination, and we decided where to portal to and the who, what, when, where, why, and the way.

If you've gotten this far in reading this book or in listening to the audio version, I sincerely hope you have been doing the exercises and applying the lessons. This is a friendly reminder that the real work happens outside the therapists' or healers' office. The real personal growth is possible when we change our reactions and apply the knowledge we have obtained. Wisdom is a combination of knowledge and life experience. Know that you have the information and knowledge. Please go out and get the life experiences necessary to live wisely and find your ultimate why.

It WERKS if you WERK it. The most important key to all these healing and awakening portals is that you have free will. You have the power to decide what portal you take and when you take it, along with the why, where, and how you take it on this self-healing and self-awakening journey. No one else can do the work for you. (Be it big or small, short or long, instantaneous or a process—do the WERK!)

You are your own healer. You are your own awakener. You have everything you need within you *now* to heal, to overcome, to feel better about yourself, your relationships, and the world. You create your world. You can shift out of an unhelpful thought process or energy anytime you so choose. In fact, there is nothing wrong with you at all. If you think you are wrong, then you are. If you think you are becoming a better version of yourself, then you are. If you think you are a badass, self-healing starseed, then you are.

You are the only one who can change you. You are the only one you really need to love and accept you. It's our relationships with ourselves that we all too often neglect. And you will never spend more time with any other soul than your own. You must go within your own inner vortex of awesomeness, and just like a cosmic washing machine you can rinse and spin the ego, iron out the kinks in your mind, and discover your soul again—just like that missing sock you've been longing to find for years.

Vision hunting for your ultimate why is like walking the labyrinth spiral of life. The spiral is a symbol of the soul's journey and a cyclical adventure you will continually revisit, bringing you deeper and deeper to inner-standing. Each cycle in life is an important stepping-stone that expands into the next. Your life will feel authentic only when you come to your own conclusions. Spend some time now journaling or freewriting on what your ultimate why might be. Go on a vision-hunting hike to one of your favorite spots in nature. Ask the universe or Source for a sign to lead you to your ultimate why and pay attention to the messages you receive. Practice using these healing-vortex-within mantras to further activate the portal of vision hunting now:

"I choose my own way forward, and I choose my why."
"I awaken my soul's desire to learn and grow beyond all existing limitations."
"I am on an inward revolution; my ultimate why will find me and guide me when I am ready."

CHAPTER 42

The Portals of R & R

> You are your master. Only you have the master
> keys to open the inner locks.
> —Amit Ray

By this point, you have learned some cool stuff about healing, awakening, and portals. Now I want to encourage and empower you to think carefully about how you want to continue to travel through the portals in this book, and any others you choose to portal through to open your inner locks. You can't live in a tornado or hurricane of healing and awakening, at least not 24-7, and survive for very long. I cannot emphasize enough the importance of intermittent R & R to rest, relax, and replenish yourself on every level; I guess that's three *r*'s!

Periodically we need to rest, replenish, and upgrade our energy *and* INNER-G, ya dig.

Energy upgrades are activating experiences of all sorts to help you replenish, activate, and shift your energy and vibration and reconnect you to your soul. They are grounded in nature and connect you to the universal forces of the earth and the cosmos. It never ceases to amaze me the healing and awakening powers of enjoying nature, getting outdoors, hugging a tree, and even going to a physical energy portal or vortex. I did just this for my last birthday on May 4—yes, my birthday is Star Wars Day, which explains a lot!

Shout out to Paul the Venetian at Mount Shasta Spiritual Tours for taking the lovely photo of me on the cover of this book at one of the *many* sacred vortices on Mount Shasta. Many authors have written about the mystical and otherworldly energy of Mount Shasta or, as some refer to it, the Root Chakra of Earth, Telos, and the lost land of Lemuria. I am no stranger to nature portals and sacred energy vortices. I was born and raised in Northern California, and we have tons of them all over the golden state. Yet none of these magical places are more near and dear to my ancient Lemurian librarian soul than Mount Shasta.

For those of you unfamiliar with Lemuria, it was a continent that existed in the Pacific Ocean thousands of years ago. Many of us old souls have deep ties to this ancient place as well as similar lost lands like Atlantis, Avalon, and Shambhala, to name just a few. Much of the work I do with my clients involves working with past lives, the Akashic records, and Starseed Galactic Origins. Through these various methods, my own research, and my healing portal journey, I unlocked significant past life memories in Lemuria and the links to Mount Shasta, where some of my family happened to move in 2017. I was thrilled to be able to visit this magical place more often, and I made an extra special trip in May 2021 to celebrate my solar return with a sacred vortex adventure with Paul the Venetian and Mount Shasta Spiritual Tours.

We spent a half day hiking all through the Ascended Masters Forest and adjunct mountain hills until we came to a very special opening circled by redwoods and rock formations. Paul the Venetian, one other gorgeous soul, and I gathered to meditate and rest among the luminous rainbow plasma-light energy that flooded this sacred vortex site. As we meditated together, enjoying the indescribable energy of this place, there was a huge influx of violet rays and bright purple light codes we all felt.

Paul the Venetian had told us about his deep connection to ascended master Saint Germaine, and we all felt that presence of divine, source-aligned energy at that moment as it strengthened our energy and created a powerful and protective force field around all three of us. I felt every cell in my body rejuvenated, and a flood of past life imagery from Lemuria came through activating a deeper and deeper intuitive sense of peace and harmony within me. Then we took some pictures, and that was when Paul the Venetian captured the photo you see on the cover of this book. No filter. This just simply had to be the book cover since it was a violet portal to higher dimensions and the best reminder ever of the replenishing forces of nature, meditation, rest, and play. Even though I hiked for miles that day, I felt deeply rested and alive again.

Now, your idea of R & R might look different from mine, and that is totally cool. We all have our unique frequency and truth on healing and awakening, especially R & R. I highly encourage you to spend five to ten minutes now and make a bullet list in your journal of seven to ten R & R ideas you know will help you feel deeply rested and alive again after all this inner work. Make sure to include some easy and practical ideas and some fun wish list ones too so you have a variety you can do on any day or weekend *and* some bigger R & R goals to look forward to as well.

I also highly encourage you to incorporate the violet flame, the violet rays, and/or a rainbow plasma light into your guided meditations or simply by visualizing them now surrounding you in a tube of rejuvenating light— just like the book cover shows. While I wish all of you had been there with me to experience it, you can experience this now in etheric form. Additionally, practice using these healing-vortex-within mantras to call in the frequency of rest, relaxation, and replenishment anytime you need it:

> "I am surrounded by peaceful energy, and I am at peace
> from within."
> "I am anchoring and grounding rejuvenating light into
> my body."
> "I choose to slow down and rest when I need to in my
> own unique way."

CHAPTER 43

The Portals of Integration and Aftercare

Integration is an act of love, not intellect.
—Abhijit Naskar

Here I go again, talking about love, but this portal is about integration and aftercare with love, of course. The path toward incension and higher states of consciousness as well as higher states of healing and awakening isn't one of light but one of balance and integration. The dark isn't bad or good. Light isn't good or bad. They are simply two halves of a greater whole. The journey of healing and awakening is essentially the archetypal hero's journey. Soul-*full* self-awareness cannot exist without the perspectives of both sides of the hero's journey. Oneness and wholeness cannot be achieved without balance and integration.

Integration at the most fundamental level simply means ownership and acceptance of all thoughts, feelings, fears, beliefs, experiences, and memories. It is about full acceptance and merging of any dissociated parts of oneself into that greater whole. Integration, much like many of the portals in this book, is a process rather than a one-time event. It is a natural process, and taking time to rest and integrate will bring a kind of peace that comes with fully accepting and loving yourself as you continue your journey. Integration improves not only our relationship to self but also our relationship to others and our relationship to life and death.

You can think of integration kind of like a well-balanced meal divided equally between the ego, the soul, the mind, the heart, and the body. All parts are fed an equal amount of healthy, nutritious fuel to keep them aligned and connected for the highest good for all. All these parts will need ongoing "fuel" and will ideally break bread together in harmony at the cosmic dinner table. When we integrate the body's energy systems we identify and release the stress or blocks keeping us stuck and causing or perpetuating a problem. This allows the body's innate natural healing abilities to flow freely, enabling the mind, body, and spirit to return to a state of balance and good health.

Why are integration and aftercare important? How does one integrate all these multifaceted portals and healing energy and the vastness of this experience? We all know how easy it can be to fall back into old behaviors or patterns after any type of healing or awakening experience. After nearly forty-four portals of healing and awakening, you might be thinking, *How the f am I going to integrate all this and apply it and practice aftercare?* It doesn't need to be overwhelming or difficult, and it will help you sustain all the wonderful progress you have made and will continue to make. Participating in the process of integration and aftercare is an active way you can continue to build on the foundation you have already built for yourself, your portals, and your healing vortex within. Like a beautiful rainbow bridge made of glitter, you want to be able to always find your way back to yourself and to use the tools and insights you have learned.

Here are some ideas to practice integration and aftercare in practical ways:

- Choose one skill or tool you have learned to practice applying every day or as needed for that week
- Take five minutes every day to review the healing vortex mantras
- Share your experience with others
- Openly accept compliments and encouragement
- Listen to others' experiences on their healing and awakening journeys
- Connect with like-minded people and communities that support your ongoing journey and do the activities that inspire you regularly

If you feel like you are having trouble with integration and aftercare, please find a local healer, therapist, accountability coach or trusted family member or friend to further support you and remember the portals of protection, OPP, and trust what feels aligned as always. You can also practice these healing vortex mantras to activate your integration and aftercare portal now:

> "I integrate what I am learning on my journey within my heart, mind, body, and soul."
> "I make time to integrate and apply all the healing and awakening lessons and insights I uncover on my journey."
> "I am honoring and exalting my healing and awakening journey through the act of integration and aftercare."

CHAPTER 44

The Healing Vortex Within and Light Codes of Consciousness

A healer does not heal you. A healer is someone who holds space for you
while you awaken your inner healer, so that you may heal yourself.
—Maryam Hasnaa

This is our final chapter and portal into the healing vortex within and
light codes of consciousness. By now, you have traveled through many
different portals within; you are more aware of your unique energy and
more connected to the frequency of your mind, body, heart, and soul.
The attitudes you develop and the actions you take create frequencies that
broadcast your essence everywhere. Cover-ups and pretense are forms of
delusion; you are who you are. You can fool yourself, but you can't fool
your frequency signature. You are always transmitting who and what you
are. This is true for everyone. Your body is loyally mirroring your beliefs
to you. The cells of your body continuously replace themselves, and in
general you don't even think about this process, yet the vital new cells
dutifully focus their attention on fulfilling your beliefs and commands.
Even though the cells are new, they will keep replicating the same old you
if you keep giving them the same old commands.

Your cells, molecules, atoms, and subatomic particles are all intelligent;
they communicate with one another because their collective job is to
respond to your input. You choose the codes of consciousness that best
express your life aims, based on the degree of awareness you have developed.
Clarity and recognition of your own power are the bottom line. Your
thoughts form your world all the time. Even though you are bombarded

with so many frequency-control vibrations that attempt to keep you from being clear, you can always fluctuate. You must make it your intention to stay very clear, stay centered, and always bring yourself back into the moment. Stop living in the future or the past and always live in your now.

Say to yourself, "What do I want? I want to accelerate my personal evolution. I want Spirit to assist me in a greater capacity. I want my body to regenerate itself. I want to embody health and wellness. I am willing to give up difficulty so that I can be a living example of what humanity can be." It is this commanding from your being and calling out what you want with clarity that brings you everything in acceleration. Practice your codes of consciousness daily. This is an act of healing, awakening, integration, aftercare, *and* incension maintenance.

You can also use the final and most creative of all healing vortex within portals now: create your own healing vortex within method(s). This is the final and most empowering healing vortex tool. Creating your own unique methods for healing that resonate with your soul energy will allow you to continue to heal and awaken yourself. If writing is your soul's calling, then *do it*! If dancing, singing, or creating art or music is your soul's calling, then *do it*! If you want to be a better version of yourself every day, then *do it*! If it's climbing a tree while wearing a disco-sequined Liberace cape, then you better do it!

Whatever your soul is yearning for and whatever the voice of your intuition is telling you to do, take action. Find a way, some way, anyway, to take some small action steps to honor your intuition and build a loving relationship with your soul. Recognize the nature of the creative force of the omniverse within you and allow yourself to take conscious steps to match it and create your own portals for healing and awakening. Remember: you create your reality, and your intuition is always guiding you to the highest good of all. Intuition is pointless without action (remember intentions and attentions or actions). Take some time now to connect with your soul and your intuition to ask this eternal part of you what unique portals you most need to create. Make a list and add to it regularly. Set crystalized intentions for each portal point on your list *and* at least one attention or action step you will take to create these portals for yourself from yourself. Say these healing-vortex-within mantras *loudly and proudly* to activate your healing vortex within *now*:

"I am creating new healing and awakening portals every
time I get inspired."
"I am my own healer and awakener."
"The power of my self-healing vortex within is limitless."

CONCLUSION

I want to take a moment to sincerely thank you. Thank you for being here. Thank you for joining me through these forty-four portals. I also want to encourage you to take a moment to thank *yourself.* There is no greater gift you can give yourself than self-healing and discovering your self-healing superpowers. When you heal yourself, you take full accountability for your life, thoughts, beliefs, and innate power. When you heal yourself, you awaken yourself to so much more than you ever thought you could embody.

Yes, it is a big responsibility to do this work, but you can handle it; for fucks sake, you *are magic,* and now you know it. You know how to heal yourself. You know how to awaken yourself. You know how to transmute triggers. You know how to play and be that awesome Electric Inner Child. You know how to upgrade your energy and even have soulgasms. You good "fo realz" now. Just keep using the tools and mantras, and when you fall off track or get out of alignment—cuz we all do from time to time—know you can come back to your soul and back to the suggestions in this book.

We need to stay connected to our souls' guidance and energy so we can learn, grow, and continue to heal throughout our lives on this earth. Our healing and awakening work is never truly done. The great part about that is that when you apply the tools in this book and harness the gifts of your self-healing superpowers, your life will become your greatest work of art.

Thank you from the bottom of my heart and the depths of my soul for entering the healing and awakening vortex within. Thank you for journeying through these forty-four portals back to yourself. I highly commend you and the courage it takes to look within and give yourself the gift of an even better you. From my soul to yours, I am sending you infinite galaxies of love and light codes and empowering reminders that *you can heal yourself.*

—Dr. Heather
Founder and CEO of Heather's House of Healing and The Starseed Sanctuary®
Heathershouseofhealing.com

Chapter 1: Be Open to Entering the Healing Portal

"I release all blocks and fears to self-healing now."

"I am choosing to enter the first healing portal now."

"My mind, body, and spirit are open to healing now."

Chapter 2: The Portal of Belief

"I believe I can heal myself."

"I am increasing my ability to heal more and more every day."

"I am choosing to believe in my ability to heal now."

Chapter 3: The Portal of Healing and Awakening

"I am healing and awakening myself more every day."

"I am open to seeing hardships as opportunities to heal and grow."

"I choose to heal and awaken myself."

Chapter 4: The Art of Portaling

"Life is art, and I am the artist of my life."

"I engage in fun and creative outlets to support my healing and awakening journey."

"I am choosing to see my journey in life as my greatest masterpiece."

Chapter 5: The Portal of Storytelling

"I choose to release old narratives and tell my story from the frequency of love and gratitude."

"I am rewriting my narrative to deeply heal and become the best version of myself."

"Stories are powerful portals that I create consciously for the highest good of all."

Chapter 6: Denial—Not Just a Portal in Egypt

"I am fully accountable for my healing and awakening journey."

"It is safe to look within at the root of my problems."

"Being honest with myself *is* healing and awakening myself."

Chapter 7: The Portal of Self-Awareness

"I connect to my personal power through self-knowledge and self-awareness."

"I choose to listen to my intuition every day and take action inspired when needed."

"I am turning the volume up on my intuition now."

"I trust the inner charge of my intuition so I don't pay the cost of ignoring it."

Chapter 15: The Portal of Intentions: Activating the Healing Vortex Within

"I am setting clear and realistic intentions for my healing and awakening journey."

"I am setting intentions for the best possible outcome for all."

"I choose to set clear and specific intentions that align with the energy of empowerment, love, and respect for myself and others."

Chapter 16: Galvanizing Portals of Abundance

"I choose to focus on practical action to galvanize my intentions."

"I transmute all blocks to abundance, and I activate abundance in all areas of my life."

"I am a galvanizing portal of manifestation for all I could ever want or need."

Chapter 17: The Portal of Protection

"I hereby void all contracts that were entered into against my free will; my energy cannot be used for anything without my conscious consent from this point forward through eternity."

"I cut all cords with anything or anyone that isn't in alignment with my highest good."

"I transmute all energy that isn't mine to hold into love; I call my energy back to me now."

Chapter 18: The Perpetual Portal of Learning

"I choose to learn from my personal experiences in life for the highest good of all."

"I am the teacher and the student; I enjoy learning and teaching from within."

"The best lessons in life come from alchemizing pain into something empowering."

Chapter 19: Time Portals

"My presence is my present."

"I choose to learn from the past, prepare for the future, and live in the present."

"I heal the pain of the past and the release the fear of the future by being fully present *now*."

Chapter 20: The Portal Less Traveled: Shadow WERK

"I am going to WERK with my shadow self, not against it."

"I choose to illuminate my shadow to heal and awaken buried treasures within."

"I am creating peaceful solutions within my personality through WERKing and TWERKing my shadow."

Chapter 21: The Portal of Luminosity: Light WERK

"I choose to honor my light within and let it guide me."

"I am a clear channel of infinite and luminous light."

"Cosmic light radiates through every cell of my body, and I awaken the dormant light within me now."

Chapter 22: Other People's Portals (OPP)

"I choose to create and maintain healthy relationships with others and myself."

"I am building a safe and supportive social network."

"Everyone is on an inner journey of some kind, and I stay in my healing vortex lane rather than swerve into others."

Chapter 23: The Portal to Transmuting Triggers, Trauma, and Tragedy

"Triggers are opportunities to heal."

"When I get triggered, I consciously pause, step back, and examine what is beneath the trigger; this is the portal to deeper healing and awakening."

"I go beyond the trigger portal to my inner vortex of alchemy and magic; I am a trigger wizard!"

Chapter 24: The Portal of Feelings

"It is safe to feel my feelings."

"Emotional pain will not kill me, but running from it can."

"I allow myself to feel; I allow myself to release and heal."

Chapter 25: The Prison Break Portal: Free Your Mind and the World

"I consciously create harmonious thoughts that help me and the world."

"I am the master of my own mind; I choose to free myself from imprisoning thoughts."

"I am building new neural pathways by choosing different thoughts; I am building a better, more beautiful internal world now."

Chapter 26: Reality Check Portal: There Is *Nothing* Wrong with You!

"I am safe and loved and grounded; I can change my thoughts and behaviors and shift dissonant energy."

"I am not my diagnosis; a diagnosis is simply a portal to deeper awareness and inner-standing."

"There is *nothing* wrong with me! I am free from self-limiting beliefs."

Chapter 27: The Hidden Portals of Healing and Awakening

"I choose to stay in alignment with my soul and the hidden realms of healing."

"I am aware of and open to the hidden portals of healing and awakening that happen every day."

"I shine my weird light bright so other weirdos know where to find me."

Chapter 28: The Portal of Electric Inner Child WERK

"My inner child is the portal to joy and laughter and feeling alive again."

"Nurturing my electric inner child is a powerful portal to health, healing, and awakening."

"The more I love and care for my inner child, the more I have access to the electric energy to heal myself and improve the world."

Chapter 29: The Portal of Incension (The Inner Ascension)

"I am now ready to move forward and shift into a higher level of consciousness within."

"I am shifting my focus on the external and going within the portal of my soul."

"I go within for all need and desire."

Chapter 30: The F-Word Portals

"I am willing to forgive my fears."

"I choose to forgive myself and others more and more every day; I create more freedom for us all through the act of forgiveness."

"I release the energy of fear on every level of my being by embracing the journey of forgiveness."

Chapter 31: The Portal of Resistance

"Fuck resistance; I choose to move through resistance."

"I choose to see any resistance I experience as insight into my fears and fuel for my healing and awakening journey. *Boom—alchemy bitch!*"

"I am dissolving resistance and avoidance by letting my higher self take the wheel."

Chapter 32: The Portal of Meditations FO DAYS

"I make time to meditate regularly in ways that help me go within."

"Meditation is an act of self-love and soul-*full* self-care."

"I choose to create my own ways to meditate and slow down."

Chapter 33: The Cosmic BreathWERK Portal

"My breath is the most powerful portal and tool I have to return to my center."

"I am choosing to breathe long, slow, deep breaths every day."

"Inhale the good shit, exhale the bullshit."

Chapter 34: The Portal to the Stars

"I make time to get in alignment with the stars and sun, and within my life."

"I am a supernova with a soul."

"I choose to see the stars in the night sky as a reminder to honor both the darkness and the light within me."

Chapter 35: The Portal of the Atomic Reframe

"I choose not to allow disasters and mistakes to define my day or my life."

"I have survived many tough situations, and I will survive now."

"I choose to atomically reframe the dumpster fire train wrecks in life that are out of my control and take my power back."

Chapter 36: Portals to Hell and Other Cautionary Tales

"I am consciously creating balance and discernment in all areas of my life."

"I choose to align with a balance of true light and true darkness, and I transcend polarization within and around me."

"I am informed and aware of potential portals to hell, and I protect myself and my energy."

Chapter 37: The Hilarious Portal: Laughter *Is* a Sacred Vortex

"I choose to make time every day to smile and laugh."

"I honor and activate my unique sense of humor."

"I am a laugh factory that raises the vibration of my healing vortex within."

Chapter 38: The Portal of Love

"I choose to love myself in practical, useful ways each day."

"I define what loving myself means to me."

"I am learning to navigate the self-love journey; I am learning to love and accept myself."

Chapter 39: The Portal of SoulWERK, Soulgasms, and Soul Boners

"I honor my soul by doing the things that light me up deeply from within."

“I am WERKing my soul daily by cultivating a loving relationship with myself.”

“I give myself permission to experience soulgasms and soul boners on the regular; I do what makes my soul ecstatic.”

Chapter 40: Unlocking the Portal to Your Unique Self-Healing Superpowers

“I have regenerative self-healing superpowers.”

“Wounds are the keys to unlocking my self-healing superpowers, and I choose to tap into my ability to heal myself now.”

“I am activating my self-healing superpowers now.”

Chapter 41: The Portal of Vision Hunting

“I choose my own way forward, and I choose my why.”

“I awaken my soul’s desire to learn and grow beyond all existing limitations.”

“I am on an inward revolution; my ultimate why will find me and guide me when I am ready.”

Chapter 42: The Portals of R & R

“I am surrounded by peaceful energy, and I am at peace from within.”

“I am anchoring and grounding rejuvenating light into my body.”

“I choose to slow down and rest when I need to in my own unique way.”

Chapter 43: The Portals of Integration and Aftercare

“I integrate what I am learning on my journey within my heart, mind, body, and soul.”

“I make time to integrate and apply all the healing and awakening lessons and insights I uncover on my journey.”

“I am honoring and exalting my healing and awakening journey through the act of integration and aftercare.”

Chapter 44: The Healing Vortex Within and Light Codes of Consciousness

“I am creating new healing and awakening portals every time I get inspired.”

“I am my own healer and awakener.”

“The power of my self-healing vortex within is limitless.”

ABOUT THE AUTHOR

Heather L. Hobson is founder and CEO of Heather's House of Healing AND The Starseed Sanctuary®. She earned her doctorate degree in Clinical Psychology from Alliant International University, San Francisco. She also earned her Masters Degree in Counseling Psychology and Bachelors Degree in Psychology from Humboldt State University. She specializes in trauma recovery, harm reduction for addictive behaviors, spiritual and existential awakenings, and holistic health methods. She deeply enjoys providing a unique and eclectic mix of both Western and Eastern philosophies on healing, spiritual awakening, ascension, and personal growth work. She firmly believes in teaching her clients how to be their OWN healers and awakeners and how to claim their spiritual sovereignty.

Connect with Dr. Heather and
Specialized Cosmic Healing and Awakening Services

If you are interested in a Starseed Galactic Origins Reading, an Akashic Records Reading, or a customized healing session by phone or video, check out Dr. Heather's website: Heathershouseofhealing.com.
On Instagram @thestarseedsanctuary
On Facebook @heathershouseofhealing
On YouTube: The Starseed Sanctuary
On Patreon: patreon.com/thestarseedsanctuary

www.ingramcontent.com/pod-product-compliance
Lightning Source LLC
Chambersburg PA
CBHW051050250726
48656CB00001B/239